Charles Henry Ross

The eldest Miss Simpson

Her haps and mishaps, her offers and engagements, her grandest success

and most woeful failure

Charles Henry Ross

The eldest Miss Simpson

Her haps and mishaps, her offers and engagements, her grandest success and most woeful failure

ISBN/EAN: 9783337173395

Printed in Europe, USA, Canada, Australia, Japan

Cover: Foto ©ninafisch / pixelio.de

More available books at **www.hansebooks.com**

BODGERBY.

THE

ELDEST MISS SIMPSON

HER HAPS AND MISHAPS;
HER OFFERS AND ENGAGEMENTS; HER GRANDEST SUCCESS
AND MOST WOEFUL FAILURE

𝔚𝔯𝔦𝔱𝔱𝔢𝔫 𝔞𝔫𝔡 𝔍𝔩𝔩𝔲𝔰𝔱𝔯𝔞𝔱𝔢𝔡

BY

CHARLES H ROSS

AUTHOR OF "TWO SINGLE GENTLEMEN," "THE GREAT MR. GUN," ETC.

LONDON
WARD, LOCK, & TYLER, WARWICK HOUSE, PATERNOSTER ROW
AND 107 DORSET STREET, SALISBURY SQUARE

LEEDS:
PRINTED BY EDWARD BAINES AND SONS.

CONTENTS.

CHAP.		PAGE
I.	THE COURSE OF TRUE LOVE AT NORTH BRIXTON	9
II.	A TRAGEDY BEHIND A PUMP	17
III.	TEA, MUFFINS, AND A LITTLE MUSIC	29
IV.	A SENSATION SCENE IN DAFFODIL TERRACE	41
V.	A VACANT STOOL AT KNOTTS AND PHLIMSY'S	58
VI.	'APARTMENTS FURNISHED'	68
VII.	MISS SIMPSON'S ROMANCE IN THE REGENT'S PARK	76
VIII.	EXTRAORDINARY BEHAVIOUR OF A SINGLE-MAN LODGER	89
IX.	PANTATTLE: A MYSTERY	101
X.	TATTYMAN IN HER NIGHTCAP	112
XI.	THE LAST OF BUGGEBY	121

THE ELDEST MISS SIMPSON.

CHAPTER I.

THE COURSE OF TRUE LOVE AT NORTH BRIXTON.

HE fell in love with her from the free seats.

She—Miss Pamela Simpson—was a parlour boarder in Miss MacSpartan's Select Establishment for Young Ladies, Virginia House, North Brixton; and, when he saw her first, was in the MacSpartan pew in Brixton church. Her eyes meeting his, accidentally, transfixed him, as it were, so that he remained standing up after the rest of the congregation had sat down; to the great scandal of the beadle, who, following the direction of Adolphus's ardent gaze, saw the whole affair at a glance. Yes, their eyes had met; but she, on her part, took no notice of him. Next minute her attention was attracted by some other object, and she thought of him no more.

The thrilling incident here described occurred just after the Second Lesson; and throughout the remainder of the morning service, and the sermon following it, he kept his eyes so perseveringly fixed upon Miss Simpson's pretty face, that, if there were really any faith to be placed in mesmeric influence, she must have looked back at him—only she did not.

He was lowly born, though hopeful, while she belonged to a higher sphere. He was, it must be confessed, but a chemist's assistant; while her papa was 'in the city,' and resided in close vicinity to Gloucester Gate.

When next he saw her, it was from the door of his employer's commercial establishment; and having his apron on at the time, he retired precipitately—only, however, to steal forth again when she had passed, and contemplate, longingly and lovingly, from between the red and blue bottles, the back of the 'white chip' which covered his charmer's head. He met her in the Brixton Road after this. She was heading the MacSpartan 'advertisement'—by which name those stately diurnal processions were enviously styled by the other rival seminaries. He was, as luck would have it, carrying a physic bottle, which he scrambled into his coat-tail pocket; at the same time rummaging fruitlessly after his gloves.

When she caught sight of him he was blushing crimson, and his legs were altogether unmanageable, as it is the nature of modest young men's legs to be, under the public eye. So weak did he feel about the knees, and so difficult did he find it to lift his feet off the pavement, that, trying to make room for the young ladies to pass, he slipped off the curb, and only by a miracle avoided sprawling.

The young lady walking with Miss Simpson, whose name was Topsawyer, giggled audibly. A smile was also perceptible upon Pamela's pretty face. As the young ladies turned the corner of the street they turned their heads to look after him, and he was still standing where they had left him, and still gazing after the young lady, spell bound, with his hat on the back of his head.

'Decidedly he is struck,' said Miss Topsawyer.

'Struck with whom?' innocently inquired her friend.

'Need you ask, my dear?' said Miss Topsawyer.

And, to tell the truth, it was not because she had any doubt in her own mind upon the subject that Miss Simpson had inquired, but just to see whether Miss Topsawyer's conceit could so far carry her away as to cause her to suppose that her own pale, pasty countenance and ugly brown bell-rope curls had fascinated the susceptible chemist.

'Don't be so absurd!' said Pamela, with bewitching coyness. 'The idea of such a thing!'

'I'm sure he looks very gentlemanly—for his class in life,' said the withering Topsawyer.

'Who is he, pray?'

'Don't you know?'

'I never saw him before, that I am aware of.'

'How very strange, and he for ever crossing your path. Poor dear youth! But I see his case is hopeless.'

'Who is he?' asked Miss Simpson impatiently.

'He is the young man at the lozenge shop.'

It was cruelly sarcastic thus to describe him, because his employer dispensed drugs and sold leeches and blisters, tooth-brushes and a variety of other fancy articles. It is true Mr. Gulphy's dealings with the young ladies from Miss MacSpartan's school were confined almost entirely to lozenges and sweet stuff. But it was not their custom upon which he alone depended, and Adolphus was not there so much to serve out paltry pennyworths of acidulated drops and insignificant three-ha'p'orths of rose and lavender lozenges, as to render himself familiar with the mysteries of 'Mixture as before.'

It was a great shame, then, thus to ridicule the honourable calling of one who, though lowly born, possessed a hero's heart and a poet's soul. And surely the fact of wearing an apron should not dim the lustre of soaring genius! Upon a subsequent occasion Miss Topsawyer spoke of him as 'the doctor's boy,' and she also, with bitter irony, called him 'Jujubes.'

Miss Pamela, for her own part, was well aware that he occupied but a humble sphere in comparison to that of a daughter of a gentleman in the city, residing in the close vicinity of Gloucester Gate; but she was rather flattered by the idea of this lowly-born but handsome hero worshipping her hopelessly at a distance. When next she saw him he had had his hair cut, and looked paler and thinner; and she thought to herself, with a soothing kind of sorrow, that he was wasting away upon her account. Perhaps, when he knew how hopeless was his case, he would go off in a decline! He might, in his agony of mind, help himself to the contents of his employer's bottles in an unadulterated form, and perish in the flower of his youth, his apron, and the chemist's back parlour. Altogether, it was very awful; but what could she do if lowly-born persons in aprons would persist in falling in love with her? Of course, there was no hope for them, for she meant to marry only for money. She had quite settled that, and many times, when looking in at a jeweller's shop, had chosen the ornaments in which she was to be presented to her sovereign.

CHOOSING THE JEWELS.

She had hitherto been in the habit of sending for her sweet stuff, and had not gone herself. It was thus that she had never seen Adolphus at his place of business. However, one day she thought she would go, and, having given the governess the slip during the promenade, entered the chemist's shop with Miss Topsawyer, and asked the perplexed assistant for a pennyworth of 'kisses.'

While he made her up a little packet of these most improperly-named sweetmeats, burning his trembling fingers dreadfully, with the sealing-wax, during the operation, she had time to observe him

THEY WATCHED FROM THE PASTRYCOOK'S.

closely. He had an expressive eye, and what people call fine eyebrows, which generally means a good deal too much of them. He had on a purple satin tie, and wore beautiful studs in the front of a shirt which was well displayed by an open waistcoat. His hair was carefully brushed and highly pomatumed; and it was, indeed, to be regretted that an otherwise noble exterior should have been marred by that dreadful apron. While he was serving her, however, in spite of his confusion he contrived to summon up sufficient courage to enter into conversation. The first words that ever passed between them were upon the subject of the weather. He said it was a fine day, and she agreed with him, although at the time it was beginning to rain. But there is no occasion to tell you

'IT MUST BE THE LOTION.'

what else they said. When next Miss Simpson went to the chemist's for 'kisses,' he with the hero's soul ventured upon a compliment which he had studied while dispensing,—let us trust not seriously to the disadvantage of the future consumer of the mixture in hand. Two of her schoolfellows, at the pastrycook's opposite, were watching them, and Pamela smiled and blushed.

This was about the beginning of February. On the fourteenth, he wrote a beautiful valentine upon lace-edged paper, and, mistrust-

WAS IT HER FAULT IF SHE WERE PRETTY?

ing the post, watched his opportunity and flung it weighted by a stone over the playground wall at Pamela's feet. The verses were very spirited; and the originality of the idea of calling her his Heart's Idol was not spoilt in her eyes by his eccentricity in spelling idol with two *l*'s. After this he wrote several epistles, some in verse and some in prose; and, in all probability, he made several copies of each, for Mr. Gulphy, about this time, could not understand what on earth became of his stationery.

It cannot be denied that, at this period, Adolphus, also, began very seriously to neglect his duties. He was for ever meditating over new sonnets, and laboriously struggling with impromptus, while making up the physic; and some of Mr. Gulphy's customers complained that what they had bought at his shop had nearly been the death of them; which arose from Adolphus's having affixed mixture labels to bottles of lotion, and being somewhat reckless with respect to the quantity composing the doses.

Now all this, certainly, was highly improper; but how, Miss Simpson indignantly inquired of Miss Topsawyer when they conversed upon the subject, could she prevent his writing to her? She might just as well, she said, as she tied her bonnet-strings at the bedroom looking-glass, have been blamed because the young man fell in love with her, or because she had the misfortune to have golden hair and blue eyes, and to be beautiful. Did Miss Topsawyer mean to insinuate that she replied to his ridiculous epistles? But Miss Topsawyer did not argue the question, and Miss Simpson's biographer has a right to have his own opinion on the subject. Pamela may or may not have replied to the poetic outpourings of her devoted Adolphus; but if no correspondence had taken place between them, it is difficult to account for some stolen interviews behind a certain pump in the most sequestered part of the MacSpartan estate.

Well, she was only eighteen; and some people scarcely reach the age of wisdom before threescore-and-ten. It is not everybody who is as wise as you and the writer, and we ought to make allowances, accordingly. Poor turtledoves! their dream of happiness is doomed to be but of short duration. Even now the horizon is overcast; treachery is at work; and Nemesis, with an umbrella, approaches with gigantic strides.

CHAPTER II.

A TRAGEDY BEHIND A PUMP.

JANE TATTIMAN was a spinster. She was thirty-five years old, large boned, and angular; being also very poor, her chance of forming a matrimonial connection was rather remote. Very early in life she had gone out teaching, and was a teacher still.

Her present proprietor was Miss MacSpartan; and, one cheerless March morning, that lady sat by her parlour fire, beguiling a dull half-hour, as was her wont, by teaching Jane Tattiman to know her place. Jane Tattiman, who had very frequently been taught her place before, and knew it, was very humble.

'Don't talk to me,' said Miss MacSpartan, Roman-nosed and majestic.

It was not Jane Tattiman's habit to talk to Miss MacSpartan. It would not have been safe for Jane Tattiman to have said her soul was her own, in Miss MacSpartan's service, or the property might have been taxed, and the tax deducted from Jane Tattiman's stipend; so, therefore, this humble person looked humbler still, and held her tongue.

'Don't talk to me, Tattiman, if you please,' continued Tattiman's proprietor; 'because I won't put up with it. You need not try to excuse yourself by saying that you did not know there were any carryings on, because you ought to have known; and if you weren't as blind as a bat and more stupider than a beetle, you would have found out these carryings on before, and then there would have been an end of them, as there shall be an end of them now; for in my establishment, Tattiman, there shall be no carryings on at all—of no sort whatsoever.'

'*You* didn't find them out,' Jane Tattiman retorted; for surely a mouse with a mouse's spirit would have ventured upon some rejoinder.

'Leave the room!' screamed Miss MacSpartan, 'and don't think that I shall suffer such impertinence in my establishment.

B

Leave the room this instant, and never dare to speak to me in such a way again. Leave the room, I say, and—come back! How dare you go like that, without even so much as a curtsey?—take care you don't slam the door, and tell that infamous girl, Miss Simpson, I want to speak to her.'

If ever in her life there was a time when Tattiman felt inclined to speak her mind, and tell Miss MacSpartan once and for all how she pitied and despised her, that was the moment; but quarrelling with Miss MacSpartan was quarrelling with her own bread and butter; and Jane Tattiman had never quarrelled with that, although she may have had differences of opinion with the nearest and dearest of her relations. She knew MacSpartan would have liked to have been able to pull her ears, as she did those of an unhappy nephew who came there to spend his holidays. Perhaps she would have gladly increased her salary for that privilege, if she had only known how to propose it.

And, after all, is not humble pie the daily food of all dependents? And who is there who does not bully some one? The writer of this work has known one of the sweetest girls to browbeat her mamma in private, and an angel of a woman to cuff and buffet her footboy without mercy. She had taken her victim from the workhouse, and he had no other friends but the overseer and the beadle, and she knew that she could box him with impunity. Ah, me! it is not every one with strong boots on who can resist the temptation of treading on a worm!

Jane Tattiman said nothing, therefore, but, dropping her meekest curtsey, went in search of Miss Simpson. That young lady was walking in the garden with Miss Topsawyer and another bosom friend, their arms twined round each other's waists like the arms of a rustic garden chair. Hearing Miss Tattiman's message, Miss Simpson coloured crimson and turned pale: for young ladies were seldom sent for except to be reproved. But after a moment's hesitation, hastily arranging her hair by the glass at the back of a pocket hair-brush, Pamela ran away to see the Lady Superior.

She ran, indeed, so fast that she was out of breath when she reached the first-floor landing, and was obliged to lean against the wall, and press her hand upon her side to stay the flutter of her heart. And Pamela's heart beat violently, too, with the fear that something had been found out; and the consequences resulting from that something's discovery must of necessity have been so overwhelming, that, after a moment's pause, the very terror drove her forward to hear the worst.

Miss MacSpartan was still seated as Tattiman had left her, with her hands in her lap, and her gold eyeglasses perched astride upon the bridge of her classical nose, looking awfully solemn and severe. Miss Simpson tapped at the door.

'Come in,' said Miss MacSpartan; and Pamela came in, trembling.

'I have sent for you,' said Miss MacSpartan, sententiously, 'because—' [Poor Pamela felt ready to faint]—'because,' pursued Miss MacSpartan, with increasing severity, 'because I want to speak to you.'

'Ye-es, ma'am,' stammered Pamela, only retaining her equilibrium by clinging to the door-handle.

'The object of my sending for you, Miss Simpson,' continued the Lady Superior, 'is to inform you that you are about to quit my establishment. Your parents are of opinion that your education is sufficiently complete for the sphere in which you are destined to move. You will be fetched away to-day.'

'Am I—am I coming back any more?' asked Pamela in a flutter.

'No,' replied Miss MacSpartan.

'Oh, my!' cried Pamela in an ecstasy.

'Miss Simpson!' exclaimed Miss MacSpartan, in terrific accents, 'I'm ashamed of you.'

'I beg your pardon, ma'am,' said Miss Simpson, becoming preternaturally serious.

Miss MacSpartan glared at her for a moment, appeared to be about to say something, but changed her mind, and said something else.

'Your silver fork and spoon,' she observed, 'together with your towels and sheets, you will leave as usual in my charge, to be—ahem—to be bestowed in charity in the customary manner. If you are desirous of giving five shillings to each of the domestics, as all

20   THE ELDEST MISS SIMPSON.

other young ladies have done before you—ahem,—I will, with your authority, charge your papa with the amount in your quarterly account, and bestow it upon the grateful recipients in the—ahem—usual manner.'

'Thank you, ma'am.'

SOMETHING LIKE A HOLIDAY.

'Stay a moment. I wish you clearly to understand that you are leaving my establishment wholly and solely because your parents are of opinion that your education is sufficiently complete, and for no other reason. Now you may go.'

Whereupon Pamela bounded out of the room; and Miss Mac-Spartan, taking off her eyeglasses, wiped them carefully and chuckled.

'After all,' said the Lady Superior when left to herself, 'that is a great deal better than telling her she has been expelled.'

Meanwhile Miss Simpson had rejoined the young ladies in the garden, and her heightened colour told them that something delightful must have happened.

'THAT'S HIS WHISTLE.'

'Are you going to have a holiday?' asked Miss Topsawyer.

'Better than that,' replied Pamela.

'Goodness gracious! What is it?' cried all the other young ladies, gathering round.

'I'm going home!'

'Going home?'

'Yes, and for good.'

'Going home for good?' echoed all the other young ladies, in the greatest excitement. 'Oh dear! You don't say so! Isn't she lucky? How happy she must feel!' Then, after a pause, 'I wish it was me!'

Miss Topsawyer at once plunged into the future. 'When do you think you will be presented at court?' she inquired.

'Most likely to-morrow,' replied Miss Simpson, carelessly; 'at least so Miss MacSpartan tells me.'

'But you won't have time to have your dress made,' said an incredulous young lady, 'will you, dear?'

'Suppose I don't want it, dear?' retorted Miss Simpson; 'suppose it is made already, and waiting for me at home?'

'How very quiet you've been about it, dear, if it is,' said the incredulous young lady, with a titter.

But Pamela had no time to quarrel. Jane Tattiman required her assistance to pack the boxes in the bedroom, and thus she was occupied the remainder of the day.

Oh, how happy she was to go home! To have done for ever with school and schoolmistresses! To have learnt the last of Mangnall and Brewer, Pinnock and Walkinghame, Tasso, Fenelon, and the rest of them! To have done with back-boards and impositions! To have seen the last of the unboltable roly-polies, and that never-to-be-forgotten resurrection pie! To be going home; to be going into the world!—how much larger than usual the 'world' sounded! To be going into 'society'! To be going, perhaps, to be married!

But what dreadful thought was it which suddenly arrested all her joyful anticipations, and caused the smile to fade from her lips and the colour from her cheek? Married! If she were married what would become of *him*—of poor Adolphus, who worshipped the ground on which she trod? Poor Adolphus! who wrote such beautiful letters, quoting Longfellow by the page and Tennyson by the half-quire (note-paper size). What would become of Adolphus—the humble assistant in the chemist's shop, who wore an apron over a hero's soul? What would become of him?

'Oh, he will break his heart—he will, he will!' Miss Simpson sobbed in an agony of remorse; 'how shall I ever be able to tell him?'

And even as she spoke a low plaintive whistle from without apprised her of the fact of Adolphus at that moment waiting for her at their old trysting-place, behind the pump at the bottom of the playground.

It was close upon five o'clock now, and twilight was fast changing to darkness. The young ladies had all left the playground for the school-room, and it was this half-hour before tea which was the safest of all others for an interview. Miss Simpson left her bedroom, stole cautiously downstairs and out at the back door. In another minute she was behind the pump.

'Pamela,' said a well-known voice in a thrilling whisper; and, looking up to the top of the wall, there, among the broken bottle ends, she saw the well-known expressive eyes and fine eyebrows—'Pamela, I thought you had gone in.'

'I am not gone—yet,' replied Pamela, 'but I'm going.'

'Not so soon, surely! It wants ten minutes to five.'

'I don't mean that,' said Pamela; 'I mean I am going home for good. I am going far away—never to see you more!'

'Good gracious! Pamela,' said a faint voice from among the broken glass, 'you—you don't mean it?'

'But I do,' replied Miss Simpson, in an awful tone; 'our fate is sealed. Don't kill yourself, if you can help it, Adolphus; and whatever you do—don't kill any one else. I'm sure I'm very, very sorry for you.'

'But, Pamela,' said the chemist's assistant, who, urged to desperation, was clambering over the wall, quite reckless of the damage the broken bottle ends might do to his wardrobe, 'you will not—you cannot—leave me thus! You will not—you cannot—forget the vows we have exchanged here on this very spot, behind this very ——'

He was upon the point of saying 'pump,' but deeming the word at such a time rather inappropriate, wound up his speech, instead, with tragic pantomime. Then he endeavoured to take Pamela's hand in his, but she gently repulsed him.

'No, no,' she replied, with great firmness, considering the painful circumstances, 'I shall never smile again; but no matter. My heart is broken; but that is of no consequence.'

'Oh! Pam—am—amela!' sobbed the bereaved one, propped up against the wall, his very legs looking limp with emotion.

He had in his last letter conjured her to fly with him from the world, though without any definite notion, as it appeared, where they were going to when they got away from it. He had no intention of taking a blue-bottle shop on his own account, nor, indeed, had he any prospect, for some time to come, of being able to do so. But he never, for a moment, connected her with the drug trade, or any of the vulgar necessities of life. She was far above all that. He would never have had the hardihood to appear before her in the character of a husband with that apron on.

'Pamela,' said Adolphus, presently, in a deep voice, which was so strangely unlike his usual interesting treble that she took her pocket handkerchief from her eyes to look at him—'Pamela, you never truly loved me.'

'Oh, Adolphus, how can you say so?'

'It is true, Pamela. Your heart is stone! You are as false as you are beautiful. If you have one spark of affection remaining for me, let us perish together!'

'Pack of rubbish!' broke in a strange voice at this exciting juncture—'don't make a fool of yourself, young man. And you, Pamela—I'm surprised at you!'

And as these words struck upon the ears of the equally-astonished pair, Miss Simpson's papa made his unexpected appearance from round the pump, with Miss MacSpartan herself at his elbow. Poor Pamela felt ready to faint, and it must be confessed that Adolphus, under these trying circumstances, showed-up like anything but a hero.

Miss MacSpartan glared evilly upon them through her glasses, and Papa Simpson,—a slender simple-looking gentleman—usually among the meekest, was absolutely terrific in his character of injured parent.

'Who are you, sir?' said Mr. Simpson, shaking his umbrella at Adolphus. 'Who are you, sir, and where do you come from, and what are you doing here?'

'I—I—I'm at the chemist's,' stammered he with the hero's soul.

'Head man and bottle-washer, I suppose,' said Mr. Simpson, coarsely.

'I don't wash bottles, sir,' retorted Adolphus, mildly.

'You'd be better employed at that than this,' said Mr. Simpson. 'How old are you?'

'Nearly nineteen,' replied Adolphus.

'You don't look more than fourteen,' observed the stern parent, contemptuously, and, certainly, Adolphus's fragile frame and beardless visage were very juvenile. 'You don't look a year older,' said Mr. Simpson; 'but if you are as old as you say, you ought to know better, and I've a good mind to—to lay this umbrella about you.'

'Sir!' cried Adolphus, shaking like a leaf, but looking very grand and terrible about the eyebrows.

'Take yourself off,' said the injured parent, 'or I mayn't be able to restrain my feelings.'

Adolphus glanced at the old gentleman for a moment as though he intended some resistance; then he turned his eyes towards the perfidious Pamela, who did not look as serious as she might have done. Upon second thoughts, he seemed to make his mind up that he had better go, and he began to climb the wall.

But, as his emotion caused his poor legs to be rather shaky, he did not get on very fast, and Adolphus's back being turned towards him, Mr. Simpson very meanly took advantage of that circumstance and resorted to violence with his umbrella. Adolphus, however, did not stay to retaliate; indeed, dropping his hat, he did not even stop to pick it up, but, having cleared the wall, ran away as fast as his legs would carry him, perhaps, to seek refuge at home, under his bed.

'And now that this tomfoolery is over,' said the remorseless parent, 'suppose you go indoors, Miss Pam, and put on your bonnet.'

Pamela did not wait for more, but retired to her bedroom hanging her head, in great confusion, while Miss MacSpartan and the old gentleman went to that lady's best parlour to settle their accounts.

26 THE ELDEST MISS SIMPSON.

Miss Simpson found her boxes packed; Jane Tattiman was cording the last when she came in, and, pausing, in her work, looked the young lady very hard in the face.

'Well,' said Tattiman drily. Pamela made no rejoinder. She sat down upon the side of her bed and, covering her face with her hands, began to cry.

'What did that old cat say?' asked humble, gentle Jane Tattiman, presently.

THE HERO'S RETREAT.

'What about?' inquired Pamela in a small voice.

But Tattiman replied only with an ominous chuckle, and went on packing. After a while, Miss Simpson looked up through her tears and took a survey of the room. 'Have you packed up everything?' she asked. 'Have you—oh!'

With this exclamation she made a spring towards the table,

caught hold of a little work-box standing there wide open, looked in and found it empty; found that its late contents—Adolphus's letters, copies of some of her own, her private diary—had all been removed. Then, with a crimson face, she turned upon her companion, who, seated upon the box she had just corded, was contemplating her very quietly.

PAMELA'S HUMBLE FRIEND.

'Has anybody been searching my things?' asked Pamela hoarsely. 'Has papa?'
'Miss MacSpartan has looked through all your boxes.'
'Through this one?'
'No.'
'Who then has dared?'

'I thought you wouldn't like the things there to fall into her hands,' replied Jane Tattiman, slowly, 'and so—and so I destroyed them.'

'Thank Heaven!' exclaimed Miss Pamela, fervently. Then in a moment, 'Why did you do that? You might have given them to me.'

'What were they?'

'A lot of letters and rubbish, and ——'

'And your diary?'

'Ye—es.'

'With all sorts of rubbish written in it. Much better destroyed, I thought, for there is no knowing into whose hands it might fall, and *in the hands of an unscrupulous person there is no knowing what harm they might do you in after life.*'

'But—but nobody did see them?' said Pamela, all in a tremble, for the manner of our humble Jane terrified her, she knew not why.

'Nobody but I,' replied the governess in a low tone, 'and your secret is safe with me.'

The single candle which stood upon the table threw hardly any light upon Tattiman's grim face and spare figure; but Pamela could see that her eyes were fixed upon her, and she trembled violently.

Just then Mr. Simpson's voice was heard calling from below: 'Are you ready, my dear? Are you nearly ready?' Pamela put on her bonnet and shawl silently. When she was dressed she turned to bid her companion good-bye.

'*For the present*,' said Tattiman, kissing her on the cheek.

Then as Pamela moved away, she clutched the wrist of the shrinking girl and whispered in her ear—

'Your secret is safe with me.'

CHAPTER III.

TEA, MUFFINS, AND A LITTLE MUSIC.

A QUIET cup of tea and a little music. This was the formula of the invitation which had brought a score of visitors to Mrs. Simpson's drawing-room upon the evening of Miss Pamela's return home. The entertainment, it was the Simpsons' desire, should be looked upon to a certain extent as impromptu, and the invitations had been issued only upon the previous day, though preparations for the coming festivities had been going on, on a limited scale, for some time past.

Every morning, for nearly a week, had Mr. Simpson carried an empty carpet-bag with him to the office, returning at night with the same bag heavily laden. Four bottles of light dinner sherry—purchased at a certain tavern in the Poultry where Mr. Simpson dined, and where being served by the prettiest waiters in London could have been no serious drawback—composed part of these loads, and six bottles of fine, fruity port; the preponderance in favour of the latter being attributable to a resolve upon Mrs. Simpson's part to go in heavily for red wine negus.

Coming home down the Strand, he bought some extra good tea at Twining's for the occasion; the 'good family' from the ordinary grocer not being deemed quite up to the mark. He, also, bought some mixed biscuits and strawberry-jam at Phythian's; where he saw so many tempting things for the table, that it was only because he had no more money in his pocket he did not buy them all.

As it was, he carried away with him a pot of Dundee marmalade, for which he had received no instructions, and, afterwards, proposed that, as it had been purchased in error, he should eat it himself at breakfast. And, as an argument in favour of this course of action, Mr. Simpson pointed triumphantly to the legend which proclaimed it to be an excellent substitute for butter; a purpose, though, to which there is no reason to suppose it has ever been applied, except by that clever old lady 'down West,' who fried a pair of soles in it.

From the Lowther Arcade he brought some glass ornaments for the piano-candlesticks, to prevent the composite from running down among the keys, as had occurred upon a previous occasion, owing to the draught caused by the skirts of energetic waltzers. There was, however, to be no dancing this time, Mr. Simpson had decided, for he did not think that the drawing-room floor would bear it; and, in fact, he had determined, as he said, not to have his house turned out of window. Therefore, no musician was engaged; but, just to keep up appearances, a porter from his office, who could be relied upon, was pressed into the service, and took the hats in white cotton gloves in the lobby, with the air of an old English gentleman welcoming his tenantry to a banquet in his ancestral halls.

'I know it's a trouble to you, Samuel,' said Mrs. Simpson when the old gentleman showed-up one evening very pale and fagged, having lugged four bottles all the way from the city, owing to its being a wet night and all the omnibuses full. 'I know it's a trouble, but then what are we to do if we don't do it?'

'Don't let's do it,' said poor Mr. Simpson, wiping his head with his pocket handkerchief.

'How you talk!' cried the lady, reproachfully, 'as if we could go to other people's houses and receive their kindness and make no return.'

'Who's been going to other people's houses?' asked Mr. Simpson, faintly.

'Bah!' replied the lady, 'that's just like you. You've no proper pride. But it's what I always complained of.'

'Well, if we must give a party,' said Mr. Simpson, much subdued, 'let's do it as cheaply as we can.'

'Nobody is more anxious to be economical than I am,' replied the lady, 'and if it wasn't for my desire to save a penny, do you think I should allow you to wear yourself to death carrying about those bottles? And, Samuel, while we are on the subject, mind you see that the negus is done justice to, and that the young men don't get together at the side table over the wine, because a bottle goes no way when there's carousing.'

'I'll take care of that,' said Mr. Simpson; 'I'll have no carousing in my house,' he continued, as he drew forth the light dinner sherry from his carpet-bag.

The old gentleman was by no means fond—indeed, he was a little afraid—of a certain genus of young man who haunted his drawing-room and found favour with mamma and the girls. Such a one at their last evening party had given him his hat and overcoat

A WAITRESS IN THE CITY.

to hold in the passage, mistaking the old gentleman, who wore a white neckerchief and a dress coat of ancient workmanship, for a manservant.

He usually felt himself rather in the way of this sort of young man, and not quite up to his standard of conversation. If he could have had his own way, he would, probably, have filled his rooms with old folks, whose claim to his consideration lay in the length of time he had known them; but whose eligibility, in other respects, was not quite apparent to an unprejudiced stranger. But Mrs. Simpson asked, indignantly, what was the good of housing such a set of people. They came there and sat bolt upright, and very silent. They ate enormously when they had the chance, and, probably, they slumbered when left to themselves in a corner, until the dancers kicked their shins or trampled on their toes and woke them up.

They had a nasty knack, too, of talking confidentially to the nice people, telling them anecdotes of the Simpsons, when they lived in lodgings in Camberwell, at a period Mr. Simpson was not nearly as well off as now.

'Yes, bless you, ma'am, and poor dear Martha—Mrs. Simpson, you know—washed the small things at home, herself, for they had no money to waste, and two young children to bring up, and very creditable of her, too, in my opinion.'

And who could gainsay the speaker? You can, therefore, readily believe that Mrs. Simpson was pleased, to think that all her superfine lady friends should be made aware of her praiseworthy conduct. Don't we all of us, naturally, fall to talking, when we make a new acquaintance, of the number of times we have had our boots mended; of the infinite service which our silk gowns have done us; turned and re-turned, dyed, darned, and cut down into under-petticoats.

But this sort of unpleasant person the old gentleman insisted upon including in the list of invitations to be sent; only the letters were not unfrequently not written, and their agreeable company thus evaded. As a rule, though, Mr. Simpson was allowed one particular guest of his own, to associate with him and keep him quiet, while the young people enjoyed themselves.

This was, generally, a fellow-clerk from Mr. Simpson's place of business (for be it whispered here, parenthetically, that Mr. Simpson was a cashier in a private bank); a person advanced in years, but, still, sprightly and lithesome in the legs; who came in pumps, and took part in a quadrille when required, or, at other times, stood looking on, smiling very blandly, even when the dancers jostled him in the waistcoat. Upon these occasions he made light of his sufferings, and said, while gasping for breath, that young folks would be young folks, and that it made him feel quite a boy again.

Several times during the evening, this ancient clerk, obeying certain mysterious winks and beckonings from the host, was spirited away into a remote corner, where he was regaled with a glass of wine, and told, for goodness' sake, to take care of himself. And though, with this warning ringing in his ears, he sometimes winced a little at the vintage, it must be owned that he did ample justice to the mixed biscuits.

Both the old gentlemen held in profound horror the supercilious sort of young man before referred to; who respected not grey hairs, and associated age with imbecility; who entertained opinions contrary to those expressed in newspaper leaders, and settled knotty points in political economy in half-a-dozen glib sentences of faultless grammar and unanswerable argument, the very unintelligibility of which was its strongest defence. A young man of this kind had one evening coolly fastened upon a bottle of very superior port, which Mr. Simpson never intended to be so treated; and, fixing the old gentleman the while, with an eye, beneath the stern severity of which the host quailed visibly, more than half finished the decanter; and then, pushing the remainder from him with a slight grimace, said simply 'sticky,' as he strolled away to find a partner for the next quadrille.

'What was it that fellow called it?' the old gentleman inquired of his brother clerk, who happened to be close at hand. 'Do you think he did it to insult me?'

'No, no, Sam, by no means,' his friend urged in a pacifying tone; 'I don't suppose he meant anything at all, and if he did I think it would be beneath you to take any notice of it.'

'If I did a half of what I should like to do,' said Mr. Simpson with determination, 'I should throw him out of the window.'

'For goodness' sake be calm!' cried his fellow-clerk, pinning him against the wall. 'Consider the feelings of the ladies, Sam; and, you know, you're not a fighting man. Besides, he is your guest, you knew; and, by the way, who is he?'

'I don't know him from Adam,' replied the host, still very wroth. 'He's no friend of mine, and I don't want his company. I didn't ask him, and I don't know who did; and—and I won't stand it.'

I dare say he didn't know who you were, Sam,' said the old clerk, 'or else he would never have abused your wine before your face; and I must say I don't think much of his opinion, for a better glass of port I never tasted.'

And, thus, the storm blew over; but this insult to his cellar or, rather, his cheffonier, determined Mr. Simpson to institute a beer jug for the future; wherein should be found that famous family ale which, as the saying goes, required but one more hop to hop into water.

It was extremely awkward for the old gentleman to be obliged to fetch his daughter from school just at the very time that he ought to have been at home, preparing himself and his house for the reception of the guests. And greatly was his loss felt during the afternoon in Daffodil Terrace; for he was very great at amateur carpentering, and was the only person upon the premises who thoroughly understood the moderateur and the kitchen clock; or could unravel the deep mystery enshrouding the ball-cock in the cistern, to which, with the aid of a flight of steps, he was accustomed to pay lengthy visits of inspection, upon Hannah Maria's assurance that there 'wasn't not no water again.'

Just as it always happens, it happened, too, that afternoon that something occurred to detain him. He meant to have had a whole holiday, but there was no one to take his place. All sorts of things turned up to keep him, and it was half-past three before he left the city. The consequence was that at the time Mr. Simpson ought to have been at home he was at North Brixton, and had a good hour-and-a-half's drive before him.

When Pamela came downstairs from the bedroom, she found her papa and Miss MacSpartan awaiting her arrival upon the first-floor landing.

'Good-bye, Miss Simpson,' Miss MacSpartan said, in freezing tones; and she took Pamela's hand in hers for a moment, turned it over, and gave it back to the young lady without squeezing it;

keeping her eyes, meanwhile, fixed upon a window on the next landing above.

Perhaps she would have liked to improve the occasion with a few appropriate remarks; but she was not quite sure that some of the pupils below might not be listening, and so she bade her young friend good-bye, and put her indignation into the pocket where she had very recently placed the last quarter's salary.

Sure enough the young ladies were all upon the watch. Somehow or other, the particulars of that tragic interview behind the pump had reached them, and they were waiting in a state of great excitement at the school-room door to catch a glimpse of Pamela on her way out.

And now Miss MacSpartan rang the bell; and Waddiman, the page, went up, with cook, to fetch down the boxes, and, together, bumped the walls and each other's shins, as they struggled with obstinate trunks round unmanageable corners. At last, everything had been brought into the passage, and Waddiman asked whether he should call the coachman to help to put the luggage into the carriage.

'Thank goodness papa has brought a carriage,' thought Pamela to herself; for she heard the schoolgirls sniggering behind her, and her heart was full of rage and mortification.

But, presently, a low, common-looking man, with a many-caped overcoat and a badge, and a strong flavour of stale tobacco-smoke, came, stumbling in, to lend a hand, and lent it with so good a will that Waddiman at the other end of the boxes flew like a feather in the wind.

'To leave in this way,' thought Pamela to herself;—'it is disgusting.' And she could hear the girls whispering together:—

'Is it true she has been sent away?'

'Who is that funny old man she has with her?'

'He does not look much like a gentleman.'

'And that horrid tipsy person carrying the boxes. He isn't a private coachman, is he?'

'No, he's a cab driver; but isn't he like the other old man?'

'Do you think so? Why that must be her father.'

36   THE ELDEST MISS SIMPSON.

'Whoever he is, their noses are exactly alike. Probably the cabman's a relation too.'

Would they never get the boxes out? Would she never be able to leave this horrid place—to get out of the sight of *those creatures?* She had had some idea of going round to say good-bye, but she began to doubt whether they would care very much about saying good-bye to her. She felt quite certain, too, that they knew all that had happened, and that she was expelled. She had told the Topsawyer in strict confidence about Adolphus; and she felt, instinctively, that it was the Topsawyer who had betrayed her. She was clever at her pencil, and would, no doubt, caricature the whole affair, and draw insulting portraits of her as Mrs. Jujubes.

MR. AND MRS. JUJUBES.

How she hated all schoolgirls! What a miserable mockery was friendship! She had some of the Topsawyer's hair in a locket, and she made up her mind to throw it away directly she got home; that is to say, not the locket but the hair. As for the locket, she might have filled it with his; but now that was all over, too. What a weary blank was the world! and would those bunglers never have finished carrying out the boxes!

'Come along,' said her father, at last.

'Good-bye, Miss,' said cook, to whom the old gentleman had just made a little present; 'good-bye, Miss, and God bless you.'

Poor Pamela! The kind words were too much for her, and she burst out crying as she gave the servant her hand. Some one, then, was sorry to lose her. Should she go back and bid her schoolfellows good-bye? She half turned with the intention, but as she did so some of the girls began to titter. It was because she had shaken hands with cook—a proceeding which no young lady who valued herself would, surely, ever think of doing. Pamela did not know the cause; but she heard their mirth, and with a quivering lip and a heart full of rage followed her father to the cab.

'Thank God for that!' she thought, as the vehicle turned the street corner, and the MacSpartan Establishment vanishing from her sight became a thing of the past. 'Thank God I have left for good. I hope I may never see any of the cruel wretches any more.'

And in her anger she forgot that Tattiman had promised always to be a friend to her. No doubt she thought that she could shake off Tattiman as she could shake the MacSpartan dust from her shoes; but Tattiman, though humble, was tenacious, and, when she got hold, it was her habit to stick like a leech.

The father and daughter rode along in silence, and the silence, to Pamela, was not a little embarrassing. Up to now, there had been no opportunity for him to speak to her about Adolphus. Was he going to do so?

She sat in one corner and he in the other. She sat as far from him as possible, and dared not for her life raise her eyes towards his face. He was looking at her, she thought. He was thinking of that dreadful scene at the bottom of the playground, perhaps, and making up his mind what should be her awful fate. And the wretched Adolphus! His fate, also, had to be decided. Would Mr. Simpson seek him out and slay him, or give him into custody? Had he done anything for which he might be transported?

And then she thanked Heaven with fervour that Adolphus had not struck her father in return when her father had struck him with the umbrella, for she had often heard the poetical chemist describe what he was like when he was roused. It was therefore a consolation to think that he had not been roused upon this occasion.

While she was thus reflecting, the old gentleman took a piece of paper out of his pocket, and began very slowly to unfold it. At the crackling noise it made Pamela's heart sank within her. Was it one of those dear letters which had fallen into the hands of her remorseless parent? She glanced towards him in silent terror, but it was so dark she could not distinguish the writing. Indeed the old gentleman had some trouble to make out the words himself by the light of the shop windows they were passing.

'What's all this?' he presently said aloud—'What's all this, in the name of goodness? Seven-and-sixpence for hair cutting! It's a wonder they left any hair at all. Why it's seven times as much as they ought to have charged to shave you.'

Pamela glanced at him disdainfully, but made no reply. To be thinking about the school-bill at such a moment—Was it not monstrous? But is it not thus that the nearest and dearest to us try our love for them? To be treated thus when she had made up her mind for something melo-dramatic; and having rehearsed her part of the Injured Heroine, not to get the 'cue'—oh, it was shameful!

Meanwhile the old gentleman amused himself as best he could in the half obscurity, by reading over items in the MacSpartan's account, and Pamela could hear him totalling up the figures— 'Seven and five are twelve,' she heard him say, 'and eight and eight—I don't quite agree with her arithmetic; but there are so many flourishes one can't make out what is what.'

Pamela volunteered no remark. She crept farther back into her own corner, and sobbed gently to herself. Papa Simpson pursued his totalling under increased difficulties, for, by this time, they had passed the shops and he could only catch a glimpse of the figures every now and then when they came to a lamp-post.

After a while, the same silence continuing, Pamela's grief grew more poignant, and she sobbed aloud.

'What's the matter, my dear?' asked the old gentleman.

Pamela sobbed louder.

'Aint you well?' inquired her papa.

'No,' said Pamela, from her pocket-handkerchief. 'I feel very ill indeed, and I hope I shall die.'

'We'll send for the doctor when we get home,' said Mr. Simpson; and then reverting to his previous occupation, 'I can't make out why they should charge me for dumb-bells if you're not allowed to bring them away. It's a regular imposition.'

It was hopeless to try to elevate such a person as this to the proper heroic altitude, and Pamela remained silent for the rest of the journey. But she made up her mind that there should be a sensation scene when they reached Daffodil Terrace.

When, at last, the cab stopped before the door, Pamela, looking through her tears and the cab window, saw, by the light shining through the blinds, that the rooms were brilliantly illuminated.

'Is there a party?' she asked, for the moment forgetting her recent sorrow.

'It's all your mamma's doing,' replied Mr. Simpson, with a grunt. 'Don't knock, cabman, I've got a key. Confound him, now he has done it!'

The cabman had already seized the knocker, and beat a loud tattoo which brought heads to the parlour windows of the houses upon either side; for the Simpsons did not belong to the same set as the Tompkinses and the Tooks, and an implacable feud existed between the female heads of the three families, which extended down to the olive branches, and led to the confiscation of shuttlecocks when an adverse wind blew down the rival areas.

Immediately following the double knock a great movement of feet was heard within, mingled with the sound of angry altercation, carried on in half-stifled whispers; and after a pause Hannah Maria, with a very red face, which had evidently been dry-rubbed round the wrong way upon her apron on her journey upstairs, appeared at the door, in answer to the summons.

But upon Mr. Simpson's voice becoming audible, confidence appeared to some extent re-established, and Mrs. Simpson and Miss Simpson's younger sister made their appearance from a little room at the end of the passage.

'It's only Pamela and myself, my dear,' said the old gentleman; 'I couldn't prevent him knocking.'

'We thought it was the visitors,' said Hannah Maria, grinning like a pagan idol, with a smut on her nose.

'Mamma, mamma!' cried Pamela, as she ran into the house. 'My own dear mamma!' and next moment she was sobbing on her mother's breast.

'Bless you, my dear,' the mother answered, gently stroking her child's soft golden hair. 'I'll talk to you presently. And you, Samuel, what a time to come home, when you knew everything would be topsy-turvy! There's no place for you to dress in, now; and something's the matter with the lamp in the ante-room; and the cheesecakes and things are all covered half an inch thick with the nasty blacks!'

And this was Pamela's welcome home

CHAPTER IV

A SENSATION SCENE IN DAFFODIL TERRACE.

You must allow that it was likely to be somewhat mortifying to the eldest Miss Simpson to come home in the full expectation of being a heroine, and then to find that there was no audience. If there is anything that could make Bill Sykes's execution, in front of the Old Bailey, a more disagreeable prospect for him to look forward to,

WHERE'S THE AUDIENCE?

it would surely be the certainty that nobody would come to see him turned off. Think of his being hanged to empty benches—of shuffling off the mortal coil and nobody to see him do it! It would really be too disgusting.

'Go upstairs and dress yourself, my dear,' said Pamela's mamma; 'it's gone seven now, and we said tea at half-past.'

Pamela made no reply, but ran upstairs to her old room, to which Hannah Maria very shortly followed her with the boxes. When she was left to herself she sat down upon the biggest trunk and sobbed afresh. But it was not for long, this time.

Why should she break her heart if nobody took any notice of her? Did they mean to treat her attachment to Adolphus as though it were all nonsense? What was there—she asked herself, with an angry stamp of the foot—what was there ridiculous about it? She could see no absurdity herself. But while occupied by these thoughts the sound of a double knock at the street door aroused her. The first visitor had come, and she must commence her toilet.

SOCIETY.

There was no time for sorrow, even had she intended any longer to give way to it. Why should she? Nobody cared what she suffered, not even Adolphus, or he would never have run away as he did—and how he *did* run! And, then, the recollection of that paltry young chemist, stuck fast upon the bottle ends, made her burst out laughing, in spite of herself; and she unlocked one of the boxes to take out her best silk, began to brush her hair, and forgot all her troubles.

SOCIETY (ANOTHER VIEW).

'They'll know I've been crying,' she said to herself, examining her reflection in the glass; and she bathed her face in cold water, powdered it plentifully, brushed and bandolined her hair, and smoothed down her ruffled eyebrows. Then—'They won't now,' she added. 'I look very nice,' she thought to herself, 'and not so horrid rosy as usual. I'm much prettier when I'm pale,' and, her thoughts reverting to the cause of her paleness, she sighed very heavily, and dabbed her eyes with the powder puff. After all, it would have been rather absurd to throw herself away on the Brixton shopman, when, in society, she might receive many brilliant offers. Her ideas about society were rather vague as yet; a sort of confused mixture of fierce eyes, cosmetiqued moustachios, sparkling champagne, and strawberry ices.

While she was engaged at her toilet, the youngest Miss Simpson entered the room, to see whether she was ready. The youngest Miss Simpson—who, by the way, was only half an hour younger, for they were twins—was not at all like her sister. She was dark, while the other was fair. She was very prim, while the other was impulsive. Her name was Penelope.

'What a while you've been,' said the youngest, taking a seat by the toilet-table, and scanning her sister's appearance with a critical eye.

'Have I?'

'More than an hour, I should think; but are you nearly ready? Aren't you going to change your dress?'

'I have.'

'Good gracious!'

'What's the matter?'

'Only that it isn't half big enough for you. How awfully fat you have grown; and how frightfully short it is behind!'

Pamela winced a little, but kept her countenance. 'It will do very well for *me*,' she said.

'Well, I daresay,' said Penelope. 'Anyhow, they'll know you've just come home from school, and will suppose you hadn't time to get a new one.'

'Yes,' said Pamela.

'I hope you won't wear these gloves, though, if they've been cleaned.'

'They're new.'

'What makes you keep them in the same box as the others? They smell dreadfully of turpentine. It's a pity there isn't time to send out for some, as those would do very well for the theatre; and you can't wear my size, you know?'

'We will go downstairs, if you like,' said Pamela.

'I wish you would let me lend you my net sleeves to hide your arms a little. How very red your hair looks by candlelight!'

'Has any one come?'

'Nobody yet.'

'I heard a knock, though?'

'Oh, that was—Mr. Stilling.'

Pamela smiled ever so slightly. It was her turn now to take her place at the wicket, and she meant to have a good innings. 'Mamma told me about him,' she said; and then she laughed, aloud, at some imaginary recollection.

It was now Penelope's turn to suffer. 'Indeed!' she said, and pursed up her lips.

'Only a tradesman's son, mamma said, but very steady.'

'Those gloves are much too small for you. You ought to buy the next size.'

'They will go on with a little coaxing. A candlestick-maker, isn't he?'

'No. A chemist's assistant!'

Poor Pamela staggered beneath the blow. *She* knew the story, then! How shameful of her mamma to betray her! They had, doubtless, all been laughing heartily over the affair, and cracking their stupid jokes at the expense of herself and Adolphus.

'I want to introduce you to Mr. Stilling,' Penelope said, as they went downstairs; 'you are sure to like him. He is so very gentlemanly.'

And then, with their arms twined around each other's waists, these loving twins entered the drawing-room, making a very pretty picture of youth, beauty, and innocence, which it was delightful to look upon.

And are you going to grumble, some of you, if the reverse of the picture should not please you? What right have you to turn the painting to examine the ugly canvas? There are some things which are intended to be seen only from one point of view. The writer of this very worldly volume stood among the carpenters, not long ago, behind a transformation scene, listening to the thunders of applause

A SWEET PICTURE.

from the house in front, and contemplating the wrong side of the 'Realms of Bliss,' and it was very dingy. After he had stood there a short time, one of the carpenters suggested that he was trespassing, and the writer had to pay his footing, which cost him a crown piece. But, perhaps, that is neither here nor there; at any rate it is not here.

Mr. Stilling's appearance was imposing, though peculiar. His hair was short and his neck was long, and he gave you the idea of a person straining to get out of reach of the sharp edge of his collar. His waistcoat was a good deal off his shoulders, and the collar of his coat thrown back, so that, when waltzing, he appeared to be coming

MR. STILLING.

to pieces. He kept an eyeglass in one eye with a persistency worthy of a better cause, and it was supposed that nothing short of an earthquake would have caused him to drop it.

He was not the son of a candlestick-maker, any more than Adolphus was a shop-boy at a lozenge shop. Surely everybody has heard of 'Stilling's Mother's Best Companion,' which answers all the purposes of a night-light, at the same time that it keeps the caudle warm, or the baby's food upon the simmer; and has been patronized, the prospectus says, by all the married royalty of Europe.

This Stilling was a whitesmith, and the uncle of the young gentleman now under consideration. The nephew, however, did not carry on that business, or any other. Indeed, when waggish people were asked what young Stilling did, they paused for a moment, appearing to reflect, and said, 'Ah, to be sure! he wears an eye-glass.' And if you inquired whether Mr. Stilling was well off, the same waggish persons, you may be sure, did not lose the opportunity of saying that there had always been a good deal of *tin* in his family.

Several visitors had arrived by this time, and were sitting about the drawing-room, nursing the tea-cups, which the bank messenger, with the air of an old English gentleman, had supplied them with, watching, the while, the younger males' manipulation of the lumps of sugar as though he thought they were taking too many, and somewhat embarrassing their movements by the fixedness of his regard.

Mrs. Simpson, to whom the absence of her daughters had occasioned some confusion and annoyance, presided with a flushed face at the tea-table, and, from time to time, entered, spasmodically, into the small talk going on around her, with an appearance of intense interest, the hollowness of which was immediately afterwards exposed by her cutting somebody short, who was weak enough to answer her random questions while she gave hurried, whispered directions to the Old English Gentleman respecting a fresh supply of muffins or another jug of cream.

'Sothern's very good in the new piece,' said Mr. Stilling; 'but I wish they would revive the School for Scandal.'

'Oh, I do so like Bulwer's plays!' broke in Mrs. Simpson. 'But who is that absurd creature—I forget his name?'

'Buckstone?'

'No, not there at all. At the Adelphi.'

'Toole?'

'No. By the way, Penelope and I went to see him the other night, and he was *so* good in that thing where he is a market-gardener.'

'Oh, *Good for Nothing.*'

A SENSATION SCENE.

'No, Claude—Claude du Val. No, that wasn't it—Claude Melnotte.'

'What, Toole?'

'Yes, we were so pleased; and tell me now, Mr. Stilling, don't you think he is very handsome?'

'Well——'

'I'm so glad you think so too. What on earth is Hannah Maria about that she doesn't bring up another plate of muffins?'

To which the Old English Gentleman replies in a stage whisper, 'I think she's takin' the 'ats.'

'Then where in goodness' name is Mr. Simpson?'

'He's doing something to the ante-room lamp.'

'Gracious goodness, with his white waistcoat on too! What a state he will be in. Ah, I'm quite of your opinion, Mrs. Mount Grampion. Give me Sir Walter for fiction. Did you ever read his Thaddeus of Warsaw?'

The conversation just about this period was rather uphill work, and it was too soon to open upon the music. Nothing else could be done then but to press all within reach to have another cup or half a cup, or 'just a little more. Now do. What not another piece of muffin? I mustn't offer you the last piece, must I? But there's plenty more downstairs. Baker, *do* see what Hannah Maria is doing. I never knew the like. What a bad tea everybody is making!'

Now some of this may, very naturally, strike the countless thousands of well-bred readers of this narrative as being rather vulgar, and the writer owns with contrition that, while he was about it, it would have been as easy to have laid the scene in Belgrave Square as in Daffodil Terrace, Regent's Park; for it is, perhaps, needless to say that he is equally at home in the gilded saloons of the proud patrician as on the modest Brussels of the humble, but honest, middle classes. However, the die is cast, and the genteel purchaser of this work who expected in its pages to encounter only the best of carriage company will, the writer trusts, find some amusement in this delineation, as a curious psychological study of a class of persons he is never likely to meet in that exalted sphere of which he is so bright and shining an ornament.

The Misses Simpson having now put in an appearance, their mamma, from behind the tea-urn, began to exchange with Miss Penelope certain telegraphic signals, full of mysterious import, dark and unfathomable.

'Whatever are you going on so about, mamma?' her daughter inquired, when she at last managed to get up to the tea-table.

'Whatever is your papa about?' Mrs. Simpson asked in an anxious whisper.

'How am I to know, mamma.'

'I'm certain I smell something curious. I hope he hasn't upset the paraffin.'

'I shouldn't think so, mamma.'

'Well, there's no knowing. He's not like any other man, or he'd never leave us here, all alone, in this way.'

'I don't think anybody has noticed his absence.'

'What nonsense you talk, Penelope, they're doing nothing else; and I'm sure there mightn't be a master of the house for all the good he's of; and I will say, if it's the last word I had to speak —— Yes, certainly, Miss Larkspur, as you say, I'm quite of your opinion. There never was a more delightful game invented than Lawn Croky.'

While this was going on, Pamela was sitting by the side of Mr. Stilling, looking very demure and pretty, and Mr. Stilling was taxing his powers of conversation to amuse her, and was succeeding admirably. Although the youngest Miss Simpson had promised to introduce her sister, as they came downstairs, it must be observed that she had no wish to do so, but had only made the remark for the sake of saying something, as they were just then passing by a couple of young men upon the landing; and that other little bit of business—the arm round the waist—arose from a similar motive. But Mr. Stilling had himself begged to be introduced, and as the Simpson family had reasons for believing that he had 'intentions,' it was only right that he should be.

Pamela knew all about him, although this was the first time they had met. Mamma had written a full, true, and particular account of how they had met him at a party at Mrs. Mount Grampion's, and he had been so agreeable, and ran out to look for a cab, although it was raining heavily. And that trivial circumstance had led to an intimacy, which had now reached a point where he looked in two or three evenings a week to tea, and, as a general rule, came the other nights to supper. It was therefore supposed that he had intentions, although he had never said anything exactly decisive; only, as Mrs. Simpson remarked, very logically, 'if he didn't come for anything, what made him come?'

'Perhaps he comes for what he can catch,' said the father of the family, doubtlessly intending to be humorous; but the ladies did not exactly understand the fun, and asked, indignantly, whether he had any fault to find with Mr. Stilling. But on this the old gentleman protested that he had not, and that Mr. Stilling and he got on capitally; although he sometimes ventured to hint, in a roundabout way, that, perhaps, the young man had not much in him, still, he always added, hastily, that he was a perfect gentleman, and (perhaps because he wore an eyeglass) that he was very high principled.

Miss Pamela sat, demurely, listening to this young man's prattle, and, as he talked, thought how very unlike he was to poor Adolphus. He was not poetical, Mr. Stilling allowed, and smiled complacently as he said so, as though he would have implied that he knew a trick worth two of that. He had read a good deal of poetry, he said thoughtfully, looking back at the profound experiences of twenty years, and he could not say he cared much about it. Not even Tennyson? No, not if he knew it. He owned he had never gone in for Longfellow, and he did not mind saying he never meant to. Pressed into a corner, he allowed that it was his opinion that a little of Byron went a long way; but he had, it is true, only tried the 'Don.'

Perhaps, comic songs were *more* in his line; but he did not care much about singing, himself. It was such a bore trying to recollect the words, and the second parts of most tunes were so jolly hard to get hold of. Yes, he was very unlike Adolphus; and yet, although every remark he made would have jarred discordantly upon the chemist's soul, the young lady listened not unkindly to Mr. Stilling's small talk, thinking the while what a very aristocratic cast of features he had, how very beautifully his boots fitted him, and how wonderfully well he held his eyeglass.

Although he knew nothing about poetry, he was very great upon other subjects. He knew a deal about billiards, and said, 'You play, of course?' to which she (pretty storyteller) replied in the affirmative. He made an old joke about 'kisses' and 'misses' she scarcely understood. He knew what was being worn, who was in town, and what set everybody belonged to. And thus, in the Terrace of Daffodil, while papa was doing the liberal with his four bottles of light dinner and his six of fine fruity, his daughter was talking '*ton*' with the tinman's heir as genteelly as the most fastidious could desire.

The only drawback to Stilling was, that he was remarkably deaf, so that even had Miss Pamela intended to flirt, she must have done it at the top of her voice. The consequence of this was, that all the room was looking at them, and listening to what they said, Penelope among the number.

'Are you fond of dancing?' asked Mr. Stilling.

'I love it,' replied the young lady.

'Waltzing, of course?' said Mr. Stilling.

'Of course,' said the young lady.

'Pity the governor won't tumble to a hop. Suppose we get up a quiet gallop while he's got his back turned?'

'How delightful it would be! But I'm afraid papa would not like it.'

'Oh, he'll take it like a lamb, if we manage him properly. It would be ever so much jollier than all these fantasias, wouldn't it?'

'A hundred times,' said Pamela, with a pretty shrug of her pretty shoulders, and a little expression of patient endurance, which suited her admirably. 'But I fear it is impossible.'

'Oh, my dear Mrs. Simpson,' said old Miss Kaffoosles—who was the only one of the dowdy genus who had obtained admission upon this occasion to the Simpsons' soirée, and only, then, because she happened, most opportunely, to have dropped in during the afternoon, curiously enough bringing her cap in paper, pinned to the lining of her gown, and had made herself so very useful in cutting the sandwiches that Mrs. Simpson had not the heart to send her away—'oh, my dear, is it a case?'

'Is what a case?' asked mamma in astonishment; and

Miss Kaffoosles, in reply, with a knowing wink, nodded her head towards Pamela and Mr. Stilling.

'Lor, no,' said Mrs. Simpson.   'He is—that is, he isn't exactly, only we think he is.'

'"MISSES" AND "KISSES."'

'Ah! I knew how it was they looked so very tender.'

'Not at all. You're quite wrong.' Then in an impressive whisper: 'He's Penelope's.'

'Oh!' said Miss Kaffoosles, with a little grimace; 'he seems very fond of both of 'em.'

And, with this remark, it for the first time dawned upon Mrs. Simpson's mind that things were not going on quite as they ought to have done. A minute later and Penelope was standing by her side, as pretty as ever; but, this time, with something of a savage beauty in her flashing black eyes.

'Do you see them?' she asked.

'Whom?' inquired Mrs. Simpson, rather weakly.

'Who? Oh, bother! How dare he do it before my very face?'

'I'll pack her off to school again, upon my word I will,' said mamma.

'You know you can't,' retorted Penelope. 'But make her come away; and, as for him, I should like to ——.'

'Hush, my darling, everybody will hear you. It is a sweet air, is it not, Mrs. Mount Grampion? Fal—la—la; Fal—la—la! You must hear my Pamela play now. She has so much improved.'

Ladies do not call their daughters sluts in genteel society, so, of course, Mrs. Simpson did not make use of the word when she addressed her eldest daughter. I am told, on good authority, that ladies are always lady-like, however angry they are. Even men don't quarrel now-a-days, and fisticuffs are as much out of fashion as hair-triggers and small-swords. We go to law now, and love each other none the less because we give one another's pockets a trouncing. If a low person should kick us, therefore, let us smile, whilst we remove the pain by a gentle friction from the palm of our hand—and bide our time.

Pamela was sent to play on the piano, and Mr. Stilling was carried forcibly to the other end of the room and introduced to an old lady. Very shortly, however, he managed to break loose, and came to turn over the music leaves.

'Why don't you go and talk to Penelope?' Pamela asked, with a bewitching smile; but still he lingered. Was she pleased that Stilling should be thus unfaithful? Who shall say? It is not in the nature of things for all of us to be happy together. While a shower of bouquets carries joy to the heart of the prima donna, the prompter is annoyed if one of them by chance falls upon and deranges the curls of his wig, which his perruquier assures him so closely resembles nature as to defy detection.

Presently she rose and began to look for a waltz upon the top of the piano, and he *would* help her. But, all at once, she recollected that it was on the what-not. The what-not stood in a second room, opening out of the drawing-room, and hidden by a heavy curtain drawn across the doorway. It was hardly a room, it was so small. You might have called it an alcove. It was a splendid place for a tête-à-tête. It had an imitation stained-glass window, this little snuggery; and a lantern outside, shining through the glass, filled it with soft and, as Mrs. Simpson said, 'ecclesiastic light.'

Pamela left Mr. Stilling at the piano and passed behind the curtain; but scarcely had she laid her hand upon the what-not, when the curtain was raised behind her, and the audacious young man stood by her side. Pamela was slightly confused, for she could not help thinking that somebody must have noticed them; and, if so, what construction would be put upon the awkward incident?

'I don't think the music is here,' said she, blushing crimson; 'never mind it.'

'But you have not looked; allow me to lift out the books for you.'

Before she could prevent him, this dreadfully nimble Mr. Stilling was down on his knees at her feet, ready to dive into a large portfolio standing on the floor.

'Could you desire a more devoted slave?' he asked, looking unutterable things through his eyeglass.

'For goodness' sake get up,' said Pamela, who fancied she heard a rustle at the curtain.

But the unhappy Stilling was too deaf to hear anything, and his back was turned towards the other room.

'Oh, pray don't!' cried Pamela, now quite certain that the curtain was moving.

'Command me, Miss Simpson,' continued Stilling, pressing one hand on his heart, and flinging at her a glance of concentrated passion through his eyeglass. 'If the devotion of a quarter of a century, or anything of that sort,—if the ——'

But here the curtain was drawn aside, and a flood of light poured in upon them.

'Tableau and blue fire,' observed a funny man, while somebody

THE PRIMA DONNA.

tittered; and Mr. Simpson's fellow-clerk, who, it is supposed, took it to be part of a charade, clapped his hands and cried 'Bravo! bravo! Very good;' and began guessing what syllable it was.

But, before long, the general consternation apprised him of the fact of his having made an error; a conclusion to which Mr. Stilling also arrived when, presently, he caught sight of the startled company, and, scrambling to his feet, let his glass drop from his eye, for the first time that evening.

THE PROMPTER.

At the same moment, piercing shrieks were heard to come from the bedroom above. Thither Penelope had fled, on just catching sight of the touching scene in the alcove; and there she now lay in violent hysterics,

CHAPTER V.

A VACANT STOOL AT KOOTER AND PHLIMSY'S.

THERE comes a time at last, if we have but sufficient patience to wait for it, when the longest stoppers take the hint and their hats, and go their ways. Sometimes it happens that the first shall be last also; such sticklers are they. But the slowest of the lot crawls away in the end; and, having given him a cheery good-night, we are at liberty to put up the chain and yawn profoundly.

After poor Penelope had been shrieking for about half an hour, and all sorts of remedies had been suggested, and tried, and found useless; when Pamela had fainted, Hannah Maria gone for the doctor, and Mr. and Mrs. Simpson were well-nigh at their wits' end; it began to occur to some of the company that, perhaps, they might be rather in the way.

Many of the ladies, however, lingered persistently; forming a sympathetic group round the hysterical Penelope, entreating her, in a chorus, to bear up; at the same time imploring each other, most pathetically, to let the poor thing have a little air; while they, one and all, crowded round, as if resolved that the quantity of the prescribed remedy which could reach the patient should, indeed, be only a little. However, finding themselves at last somewhat rudely jostled by the paternal Simpson, they presently cleared off, by ones and twos, taking their male belongings with them, and registering vows upon their way home never more to set foot within those low people's house.

Some of the single gentlemen then strolled away. Three young ladies, whose cab had been ordered for a much later hour, sat with their opera-cloaks on, in the drawing-room, waiting until some good soul could be found who would fetch them another vehicle. These, with the exception of two gentlemen, were the only visitors left; and the two gentlemen were the ancient clerk and young Stilling.

Now the rich part of the business was, that Stilling had not a notion that his perfidious behaviour had been the cause of all the mischief. This high-spirited young simpleton had looked upon the alcove catastrophe as rather a good bit of fun. He had no idea that Penelope's hysterics had therefrom arisen, or that it was such a serious attack; and he was not aware that everybody was rapidly taking their departure.

The old clerk was also in the same state of blissful innocence; and they sauntered downstairs together, and found some wine and sandwiches upon the parlour table.

'This,' said young Stilling gaily, 'is considerate.'

'And timely, sir,' said the old clerk, who felt peckish.

'We'll take a snack, if you have no objection,' said Mr. Stilling.

'None in life, sir,' responded the old clerk; 'may I assist you to a glass of sherry?'

Mr. Stilling was open to the offer, and would be proud to take wine with him.

As there was, as Mr. Fondilove facetiously remarked, 'no extra charge,' they took a chair while taking their wine and sandwiches, and made themselves comfortable, in a small way. Surely, such conduct was natural enough; but mark the terrible results.

An amusing young dog was that Stilling, when he tried, and the old clerk was a man who could appreciate a good joke. What, then, was more natural than that, when Mr. Stilling gave a highly ludicrous account of a tipsy freemason making an after-dinner speech, Mr. Fondilove should lean back in his chair and roar with laughter. Finding his comic efforts thus appreciated, what more natural, then, than that Mr. Stilling should elaborate his humour, and, to give character to the impersonation, turn up one side of his collar, drag his necktie awry, and jerk his coat off one shoulder?

But, at the same time, it is not to be wondered at if Mr. Simpson, coming suddenly into the room whilst Mr. Stilling was swaying to and fro with a wine-glass in his hand, and not being acquainted with the circumstances of the case, should come to a hasty conclusion, and suppose that Stilling—the miscreant Stilling,—in this, the moment of his innocent victim's suffering, was carousing upon his, the injured father's, wine and sandwiches.

The misguided Fondilove, unconscious of wrong-doing, was leaning back with his chair up against the wall, and he, also, had a wine-glass in his hand, and was, evidently, enjoying himself immensely. But, at the sight of Mr. Simpson's solemn face, he brought his chair down upon its four legs, and sat motionless; his wine-glass in one hand and a sandwich in the other.

Mr. Simpson glared upon the bacchanalians with a terrible expression, and, leaning across the table, clutched at the decanter.

'I didn't think it of you, Bob, by heavens!' he said, in a choking voice. 'I shouldn't have looked for it from you, I really shouldn't!'

'I hope I've done no harm, Sam?' said Fondilove, plaintively. 'What the dickens is the matter?'

'The matter!' cried Mr. Simpson, much excited, 'Ha! ha! Nothing!' and then he added, with a wild attempt at harmony, 'Push around the bowl, for he's a jolly soul. Go on; why don't you push it round?'

It dawning upon Fondilove that his old friend Simpson was displeased at finding him refreshing himself, he became immensely embarrassed by his handful of sandwich, and would, had he seen a way of doing so unobserved, have hidden it away in his pocket. Young Stilling, too, reflecting upon the extraordinary appearance that he must have presented when imitating the tipsy freemason, was anything but comfortable.

'I don't want any more, thank you,' he said, as Mr. Simpson pushed the decanter towards him.

'Don't mind me, sir,' said Mr. Simpson, 'I won't be a death's-head at the feast. What matter if my child is suffering? What odds if the happiness of my home's blasted? Let us carouse. Bob Fondilove, I call upon you for the next song.'

Suddenly a light broke in upon the old clerk, though, unfortunately, it was a wrong light.

'Sam, old man,' said he, 'I never saw you taken this way before. I always thought you'd a head like a rock.'

'This way!' repeated Mr. Simpson, wildly; 'what way?'

'Don't take any more, Sam,' said Fondilove, laying his hand upon his old friend's arm as he was about to help himself to a glass. 'Be persuaded, old man. You'll be so bad to-morrow.'

'I'll be bad now, perhaps,' said the old gentleman, 'if I have much more of it.'

'That's what I say,' cried Fondilove, eagerly; 'don't drink any more.'

'What!' gasped Mr. Simpson, 'do you mean to say—But, damme, I see now. They're both of them one as bad as the other. Look here, gentlemen; hospitality's hospitality, but it may be abused; and I shall be glad to wish both of you good evening.'

'By Jove, I say,' cried Stilling, half angry and half frightened; 'I say, you know, by Jove, I say!' and he looked appealingly towards Fondilove.

But the old clerk made no answer. He had known his friend Sam some forty years and more, and he never thought to have been so treated. He could not imagine why he was angry; but he was too high-spirited to ask. One thing he understood plainly enough, and that was that he was turned out of the house.

'Good evening, sir, good evening,' he said, as he moved to the door, 'I won't intrude again, sir, depend upon it.'

As he spoke he nervously twitched at the buttons of his coat, vainly to fasten it across his breast. 'Thank you, Baker,' he said meekly, as he took a hat for which his had been changed by mistake, and which was some sizes too large for him, and toddled out into the rain.

Before he had gone many yards Stilling overtook him.

'Precious like a dirty kick out that was,' observed the young man.

'I wish Sam had kicked me,' observed the old clerk, despondingly; 'I shouldn't have been more hurt.'

'Well, I won't go as far as that,' responded young Stilling. 'Boots off, as the bootjack said. Old Fireworks must have been tight. Don't you think so?'

'I have known Sam,' said Mr. Fondilove, taking his companion by the button and holding him at bay by the side of a lamp-post. 'I have known Sam, man and boy, this ever so long. I knew Sam, bless you, before he came to our place—that's the bank, you know,—and I was his best man when he was married; and I'm the godfather to the twins. If I hadn't gone rather too deep into building specs, which didn't turn out quite as they were expected to do, I should be pretty warm just now; but, I won't deceive you, I'm not.'

'It is rather chilly,' said Mr. Stilling, turning up his coat collar.

'That's neither here nor there, though,' continued Fondilove, without noticing the interruption. 'I feel his treatment deeply. If I were well off, though, I should not care. If I were not under an obligation to him it would not matter. But he has lent me his name, Mr. Stilling, and I can't take it up right off as I should like to do. I've lent him my name before now; but, as bad luck will have it, it's the other way this time. It only wants a week of renewing, and it —it cuts me to the quick.'

'I don't know anything about quicks,' said Stilling; 'but I tell you what, if you don't pretty quick get home you'll get your death of cold. Mark my words if you don't. Good-night.'

He tore himself away with this, and left poor little Fondilove under the lamp. When he was alone he leaned his head against the post and groaned; but a policeman passing by and catching sight of him, took him by the arm and asked him whether he knew where he lived.

'Yes, I know,' replied the old clerk, looking at him absently. 'In Clement's Inn.'

'Better get home, then,' remarked the policeman, with a grim smile, 'unless you want a lodging at a half-way house.'

Fondilove waited for no more, but shuffled off in a southerly direction. It was raining very fast now, and when he drew up in the Hampstead Road and looked round for a cab he was wet through.

The last yellow omnibus came up while he was waiting. There was room for one inside, and he got in. All the way to the Strand he shivered miserably, and when he got out, at last, by St. Martin's Church, his teeth chattered with the cold. He hurried home as fast as he could, but he could not warm himself. He would have made a glass of hot grog, with the aid of his bachelor's kettle, but he was out of wheels. In lieu thereof, he took a dram neat, tied a stocking round his neck, and crept into bed.

Next day Fondilove's place was vacant at the office. Mr. Simpson many times looked, uneasily, in that direction, wishing for and yet dreading his arrival. During the afternoon a letter came for one of the heads of the firm, to say that the old clerk had a bad cold and regretted that he was unable to attend to his duties.

'A cold, he calls it,' said Mr. Simpson to himself, with a chuckle.

The next day, and the next, however, passed away, and yet Fondilove's perch remained unoccupied.

'I wish you'd go and look him up, Simpson,' one of the partners remarked to their cashier; 'the poor fellow must be seriously ill, or he would never stay at home in this way.'

But Mr. Simpson did not relish the notion of a visit, after what had occurred. He was trying to think which of the other clerks he could persuade to undertake the business in his stead, when a letter arrived by the post.

'Dear Sam,' it said, 'I am very ill, and they say not likely to get over it. For the sake of old times, come and see me once more. Your old friend, ROBERT FONDILOVE.'

Sitting with this letter spread before him upon an open ledger, a strange dimness came over Mr. Simpson's eyes, which had nothing whatever to do with his spectacle-glasses.

Just at that moment, he was not any longer head-cashier at Kooter and Phlimsy's; but a rising young clerk, on a salary of sixty pounds a year. He had got all his hair back upon his head; not grey, though, but light auburn, as it used to be. He had lost considerably in the width of waistcoat, and was, generally, much slimmer. The world was, at least, thirty years younger, and, dear heart, how many centuries more innocent and hopeful!

Bob Fondilove, too, was young and sanguine. He had his way to make; but, egad, he meant to make it. There was no difficulty big enough to block up Bob's high-road to wealth and fame. Oh, he was a deuce of a fellow, was Bob, thirty years ago; and no connection whatever with the grey-headed, bent, and wrinkled old gentleman whose stool stood, over yonder, vacant.

Thirty years ago! That was before he went a-courting. Why, it was not more than twenty years ago when he was on his honey-moon. Martha was not quite so podgy then; and, perhaps, her temper was more desirable. Why, she must have been very pretty. Yes, he was sure she was. On their wedding tour—Gravesend was at the sea-side in those days, or, at least, people bathed there—even the waiters, at the hotel, nudged one another as she passed, in evident admiration. He recollected all that, and events that happened ten years before.

Thirty years! and yet it seemed like only yesterday. To think that he had got thirty years nearer death, and done so little!

AT GRAVESEND.

When the bank closed, at four, and the books were balanced, there was a mistake of a penny, which it took the united arithmetical powers of the office nigh upon forty minutes to account for; for nobody suspected the head-cashier to be capable of making a mistake in addition. As, however, it was customary at Kooter and Phlimsy's, as at other banks, to wait until the mystery was cleared up, the younger clerks waited, chafing in spirit; and from that day may be dated the impression, which gained ground steadily among the juniors, that old Simpson was breaking up, and ought, very speedily, to be pensioned off and put away upon a shelf.

When the great penny difficulty was settled, to the general satisfaction, the head-cashier took his way along Cheapside and down Fleet Street to Clement's Inn. His friend Fondilove inhabited a dreary little third-floor room, singularly dark and misshapen; the ceiling sloped in several directions, while even the floor had a sort of hill in it, which was a source of constant surprise and discomfiture to unwary visitors; while tables placed on firm ground, as regarded three legs, were discovered, upon pressure being applied to them, to be balancing a fourth leg in the air in ballet fashion.

Opening out of this room was a sort of cul-de-sac, or blind alley, which had, probably, been a passage, until a doorway at the end of it had been bricked up; and here, in a grim obscurity, Mr. Simpson found his old friend in bed; and found him horribly changed.

'It's very good of you to come, old man,' was Fondilove's greeting, in what he tried hard to make a cheery voice, but it was very cracked and tremulous.

'I had no idea you were so ill, Bob—old fellow.'

'No—no; how could you, Sam? Or else you would have come. I knew very well it wasn't anything else kept you away ——'

'Of course, it was nothing else,' said Sam, with something like a blush, which the darkness of the room, fortunately, concealed.

He had not quite got over the feeling of resentment at what he thought to be such unfeeling conduct on the part of his old friend; but, seeing him lying here stricken down, he made up his mind to forgive him.

On his side, Fondilove had not forgotten Sam Simpson's cruel rudeness; but, attributing it to drink, he, also, had made up his mind to let bygones be bygones. And thus they thought, as they shook hands here, upon the brink of the grave; and yet the cloud which had come between them, and which a word could have dispelled, remained between them to the end of time—for the word was never spoken. After a short pause, Fondilove continued—

'I wanted to see you, Sam, about—about that bill. It comes due in a day or two, you know.'

'Ah! to be sure,' replied Simpson thoughtfully. 'So it does—in a day or two.'

'When it is presented, Sam, I—I sha'n't be here, I'm afraid.'

The other looked at him hard, and was silent. He had, for a moment, a vague idea that Fondilove meant to bolt. Slowly, however, the truth dawned upon him.

'You're not as bad as that, Bob,' he said, in a trembling voice; but looking into the wan wasted face before him, he saw that his old chum was speaking the truth.

'Yes, I am, Sam; but don't take on on my account. I'm ready, if it was not for what I've got on my mind. With all that's due to me at the office, Sam, you won't make more than sixty pounds, and that will leave a hundred and ten pounds unpaid on the bill. I meant to have paid off another thirty again this quarter. I—I never counted on dying and leaving you in the lurch.'

'Don't fret about that,' said his friend, taking his hand again. 'We've helped one another, Bob, before now. You'd have done as much for me, if I had asked you. It can't be helped, Bob—don't let it trouble you a bit. Besides, you'll be well and strong again, yet. Why, you're worth two such as me—I'll lay my life on it!'

He said as kind and cheering things as he could, and sat some hours by his friend's bedside. They talked very little, for the sick man's voice was so weak that at times it was scarcely audible. Now and then, though, the old clerk would call him to his side, to ask whether he recollected such and such a thing that happened many years ago.

He seemed to be, in those few hours, living over again the days of his youth; and, more than once, he mentioned names of men who were long since dead, and of firms that had ceased to exist. Several times he fell off into a gentle sleep—at other times he was so still and silent that his friend, half terrified, would bend his head low to the grey quiet face, and listen intently for his breath.

Towards midnight, Mr. Simpson decided that he must go home, or his family would be alarmed. He had sent for a nurse, who had just arrived; and he stooped down over the invalid to bid him good-night, and to promise to call early in the morning; but poor Bob Fondilove would never hear that well-known voice again. Death had stolen upon him, gently, in his slumber, and he awoke no more in this world.

After a while Mr. Simpson was sufficiently himself again to take his way home through the lonely squares. Perhaps, once or twice, he might have paused, in the loneliest places, to wipe away a stray tear that was wandering down his cheek.

There are not many men's friendships that pass the middle age. Senility affects the company of youth, which, anyhow, respecting age much more than age respects itself, is docile and pliant, and listens patiently. There are few more ghastly shams than jolly good fellowship; and, after a time, when we have found one another out, we join in that jovial chorus less and less heartily, until we drop out of it altogether.

CHAPTER VI.

'APARTMENTS FURNISHED.'

IN the vicinity of Gloucester Gate patrician mansions proudly rear their stuccoed fronts. There are terraces thereabouts where only carriage people would think of residing, and where servants in livery are as common as blackberries.

But just round the corner, as it were, you come to less-imposing edifices—though, still, highly genteel. Nothing, indeed, looked at from a Daffodil point of view, could well be genteeler than Daffodil Terrace.

There was no vulgar public-house at the corner, and no shops, not even a brass door-plate in the row, to indicate the existence of a professional person. At more than one of the houses they kept a real live boy in buttons, and, while they were about it, on the score of buttons, used no niggardly hand.

Quite frequently—several times a week—carriage company made calls upon Daffodil Terrace; on which occasions the thundering rat-tat-tats that announced the arrival of these distinguished visitors brought heads to all the other parlour windows down the row; though the writer must not omit to mention that the greatest possible pains were taken by those heads' owners to keep them hidden behind the window curtains.

There, perhaps, never was a terrace within six miles of the Bank with such clean door-steps as that of Daffodil, or such very tidy servant-girls, in such uncommonly smart cap ribbons. There, certainly, never was a terrace which kept up such an appearance on as small an expenditure; and, whatever desperate struggles there might have existed within the bosoms of its families to make both ends meet, not a glimpse did the outer world obtain of these little pinchings and screwings practised by stealth, with double-locked doors, far beyond the ken of the ever-vigilant Grundy.

In such a terrace, then, how could a genteel family let lodgings without a loss of dignity? It was a difficult matter; and, yet, it must be tried. Mr. Simpson had clearly proved to the wife of his bosom that either the household expenses must be retrenched, or an addition made to the family's income. There were a drawing and a bed-room which could be dispensed with; why not try and find a quiet, single gentleman, or, better still, a boarder who was willing to join a cheerful musical family circle, and would pay handsomely for that privilege?

The question was, how was it to be done without the dreadful secret becoming known to the rest of the Terrace? It had been tried by others. An advertisement had appeared in one of the daily

A MOST OBLIGING FANCY STATIONER.

papers couched in these terms:—'A lady, whose house is larger than she requires, is desirous of meeting with another lady willing,' et cætera. But the Terrace had looked upon this as a shallow pretence, and the finger of scorn was, pitilessly, pointed at the poor pretender.

The unfortunate person alluded to had given the number of her house in the advertisement; truly an injudicious proceeding, and, taking warning by her fate, another speculator had said, simply, 'Furnished Apartments in Daffodil Terrace. For cards to view, apply to Mr. Figgs, Grocer, Praed Street, Camden Town.' But, woe unto him! Other persons from the Terrace dealt with Figgs, and the secret circulated extensively.

What was to be done? At length a bright idea occurred to Mr. Simpson. A young fancy stationer in the neighbourhood, who had just started in business (Miss Penelope had dealt with him some time for the *Quiver* and *Sunday at Home*), was most anxious to do all he could to please his customers. A handsome card, on which the words 'Furnished Apartments' were boldly engraved, having been purchased at his shop, he, when appealed to, expressed a willingness to have it placed in his window, where he, also, allowed it to occupy a prominent position, to the total extinguishment of a small pile of sixpenny water-colour boxes.

Mr. Simpson, however, not entering with much interest into the paint-box question, was highly delighted with the way in which his card had been placed, and the news having been imparted to Mrs. Simpson, the lady and her two daughters were even tempted to take a little promenade in that direction, and, passing rapidly in front of the fancy stationer's, cast a sidelong glance as they went, which took in all the particulars.

'Nothing,' said Mrs. Simpson, 'could be more satisfactory.'

An unfortunate occurrence, however, upon the afternoon of the following day, caused the family to alter their opinion.

The young ladies had been for a stroll in the Regent's Park, and on their way home, not being very distant from the fancy stationer's, they passed that way just to see how the card looked, and looking very hard could see nothing of it. Under these circumstances, having passed by the shop a few yards, Pamela proposed that they should retrace their steps and look again, which, with a pretty affectation of having forgotten something, they did, but with no better success.

'Mamma,' said the eldest Miss Simpson, in great excitement, the moment the street door was opened, 'have you done it?'

'Done what?' asked Mrs. Simpson in astonishment.

'Have you let?'

'Lor bless me, no, my dear.' And hereupon followed an explanation.

'Your papa shall see about it when he comes home,' said mamma; and as soon as Mr. Simpson arrived he was sent out to make inquiries.

'He was searching after a water-colour box and knocked the card over on its face,' explained the head of the family, on his return. 'Of course I could not say much, you know, for it is very good of the man to let it be up at all.'

'Oh, certainly,' said the young ladies; and they all tried to look as cheerful as possible.

But next day there was another misfortune.

'Mamma,' said one of the young ladies, coming in from another stroll in the Regent's Park, 'that horrid card is gone again.'

'You don't mean that?' cried Mrs. Simpson.

'Yes, we do, and it's worse this time.'

'Worse?'

'Ever so much worse. It hasn't tumbled over. It's out of the window altogether.'

The news being reported to Mr. Simpson, he said it looked bad, and, moreover, it was rather awkward.

'I can't keep bothering the man,' he said. 'However, I'll go round and buy a packet of envelopes and see what can be done.'

Half an hour afterwards, returning again, Mr. Simpson said that a new course of conduct must be adopted. It would seem that the fancy stationer had gone to town early that morning, leaving his wife in charge of the shop. A person had come in and asked for a card of 'furnished apartments.' The fancy stationer's wife had made a search, and replied that she was afraid they were out of them.

'There's one in the window,' the customer remarked. 'So there is,' said the fancy stationer's wife, and, not being aware of the arrangement her husband had entered into, she sold the card; and the purchaser, departing in triumph, hung up his advertisement somewhere in the neighbourhood; 'and for what I know to the contrary,' said Mr. Simpson, 'he has potted our lodger, that ought to have been, with our own card.'

Upon receipt of this intelligence, the countenances of the three ladies looked rather blank, and a council of war was held over the tea-table.

'There's nothing, in my opinion,' said Mr. Simpson, 'as good as a bill in the window.'

'How ever can you talk like that?' cried Mrs. Simpson, indignantly. 'As if you wanted all the world to know about it.'

'As long as we can manage to make one of them know it, I sha'n't care,' said the old gentleman; 'but don't it strike you that

THE EQUESTRIAN LODGER.

we are rather like that reduced gentlewoman who wanted to sell matches and was afraid to speak up?'

'I can't think how you can be so low, Sam, to talk about matches; as if you wanted the children to think there was something degrading in letting a portion of one's house, for which one has really no occasion, when it can be done nice and quietly without anybody knowing anything about it.'

'Exactly,' said Mr. Simpson.

That something must be done was very evident, and, after all, an advertisement in a newspaper seemed to be the best method.

AN INVALID LODGER.

Mr. Simpson, therefore, with the ladies' assistance, drew one up and took it to town with him next morning. Some days elapsed before it was inserted, and when it did at last make its appearance, although all four made a search, they all four failed to discover it. The consequence was, that Mr. Simpson called at the newspaper office to complain, and had the advertisement pointed out to him.

'I only hope,' said the old gentleman, on his way home, 'that people who don't feel quite so much interest in the matter as we do may be more clear-sighted.'

Several persons seemed to have discovered the advertisement, and wrote to the address given, to know where the apartments were to be found, and what the terms were. Some of those inquirers, however, did not give their own names and addresses, but wished the letters to be directed to certain initials, and these, the Simpsons —suspecting treachery from the Terrace—did not reply to.

Others again were so flippant in their tone that, although they were answered, the Simpsons felt certain it was a mere waste of stamps and stationery. One, who was kind enough to inform them that he kept his own cab, wanted to know whether there was stabling for two horses, which, Mr. Simpson could not help thinking, was an unusual appendage to two furnished rooms. One was an invalid, whom four doctors attended, and whose lapdog alone would, seemingly, have necessitated keeping a second cook. And one, a lady, whose spelling was indifferent, wrote as though the affair were quite settled, saying, 'I shall probably want it for a long period. You must, however, find me another apartment for my ayah. I shall dine at home, and occasionally receive company, when I shall want the use of a second drawing-room.'

Reading this letter through, Mrs. Simpson observed, in a general way, 'I wish she may get it;' and presently added, 'we don't want any ayahs in this house, thank you;' and, from a subsequent remark, it would almost have seemed as though she looked upon an ayah as some sort of wild quadruped of a dangerous character. In answer to the most likely applications, Mr. Simpson wrote elaborate replies, touching upon the salubrity of the air, the gentility of the neighbourhood, and the facilities for divine worship. The elegance of the composition excited justifiable pride in the bosom of its author and its author's family; but the chronicler of those events regrets to add that not the slightest notice was taken of Mr. Simpson's letters, and, after waiting a week, it was thought advisable to advertise again.

In the meantime, however, the eldest Miss Simpson happened to take a walk in the Regent's Park, from which apparently trivial circumstance came the most startling events. Among other extraordinary results was Spring Green, who surely deserves a chapter to himself.

CHAPTER VII.

MISS SIMPSON'S ROMANCE IN THE REGENT'S PARK.

BECAUSE our young friend Stilling has rather quietly glided out of this history, it must not be supposed that that affair of the alcove was forgotten and forgiven all in a moment.

Of course, Pamela justified herself; indeed she did so with some vehemence. She had given Stilling no encouragement, she vowed and protested. Besides, after all, he was only on his knees looking for a music-book. And then, Mr. Simpson, himself, had proved him to be under the influence of strong drinks.

The affair being talked over, and certain explanations having been made, the conclusion arrived at by the ladies was that Mr. Simpson had been a deal too hasty. Mr. Stilling was very young, and his head was notoriously weak. Boys would be boys. It was not every one in the world who was capable of resisting the temptation of the fine fruity. One glass led to another, and some gentlemen are so easily overtaken. His conduct was decidedly wrong; but surely not unpardonable.

Ah! who can plead for us wrong-doers like dear, forgiving woman? It struck Mrs. Simpson that young Stilling was far too good a match to be flung away thus lightly. Supposing, thought the prudent mother, he had preferred Pamela to Penelope. Well, Pamela would then have been provided for, and it would have been Penelope's turn next. But if it were true, as the young lady herself protested, that Pamela detested the sight of him, a little clever generalship might have brought him back to Penelope's feet.

It really might have been arranged so nicely, either way, if that stupid blundering old father of the family had not turned the young man out of doors.

Of course they had not the remotest notion that Mr. Simpson had made the blunder he had, and that young Stilling was not tipsy at all; so, perhaps, it was not very considerate to poor papa's feelings to suggest the course which, after much debate, was thought most advisable. It was decided that young Stilling should be forgiven; and, as he would not come there to receive pardon—they had seen nothing of him since the fatal evening,—it was proposed that Mr. Simpson should go and beg the young man's pardon. To see the expression of the worthy old gentleman's face when this idea was delicately broken to him was to see a sight never to be forgotten.

'I'm damned if I do!' said Mr. Simpson, from whose mouth so wicked a word had not come this many a day; and the females of the family, awed by this terrible outburst, dropped the subject.

Poor Penelope! She did not very quickly forgive her sister; but, doubtless, the thought that both had lost him, and that Pamela's piratical cuttings out had done her no service after all, may, to some extent, have soothed her wounded feelings.

Penelope was pretty, but pale and thin; and, indeed, rather what may be termed whispy. She had not the style about her that her sister had, and she had not a great deal to say for herself. A certain prim and perky demeanour, which this slim maiden thought fit to adopt towards he-creatures, generally, frightened the bashful sex rather than encouraged it.

Few young men having been snapped at, and bounced at, and put down, and kept in their places, during the first interview, cared about trying it on any further. Stilling may have protected himself behind his eyeglass, as behind a shield, for he had been very venturesome, and, evidently, had intentions.

Pamela, on the other hand, as we have seen, inspired love upon very short acquaintance, or, indeed, upon no acquaintance at all. She was very pretty, was Pamela.

Her enemies were wont to assert that her hair was red, and not golden. It could not be denied that it had a reddish tint about it; but its owner, in those days, indignantly denied the fact. Subsequently, public taste having changed, and red hair being suddenly discovered to be anything but hideous, Miss Pamela insisted upon her redness.

She had very beautiful eyes, that could fascinate you, or wither you, as was her wish. She had such pretty roses on her soft cheeks. She had a proud carriage of her head, and a majestic sweep of skirt,

There, surely, was no young woman alive who could have got the amount of swish and rustle out of a dyed black silk.

There, surely, was no other young woman who wore such pretty boots; though, seeing that boots cost a deal of money, and her papa was anything but well off, how she managed it was an everlasting mystery.

AT BRIGHTON.

She was not, it must be confessed, an industrious young person: and a piece of needlework assumed a grimy aspect under her fingers, pretty fingers though they were. How then account for tho wondrous depths of embroidery upon her under-garments, which the improprieties of rude Boreas, or a praiseworthy desire to save the hem of her outer garment from the dirt, at times revealed to the most fortunate of mortals. Begged, borrowed, or stolen, thero it was; for it could hardly have been bought upon the small allowance on which Miss Pamela somehow contrived to dress herself

PAMELA'S BOW.

so becomingly. And, ah me! when there came a time when silks and satins were more plentiful, you should have seen her, as the writer did, one season, at Brighton. There was no stint of *moiré* about that train of hers!

She was, indeed, a very bright and pretty young lady, at whom the male dwellers in the Terrace stared admiringly; whilst the women, though staring if anything harder than the men, may perhaps have been, on the whole, less enthusiastic. She was just that sort of young lady that men must fall in love with whether they wish to do so or no; not that, by the way, they ordinarily struggle hard against such a misfortune.

Young Tompkins, next door, was decidedly smitten, and proposed to his mother and sisters that they should bury the hatchet and end the long and deadly feud which had been going on between them and the Simpsons any time these five years past. It was the same with young Took, next door on the other side; and old Took even went so far as to say that the Misses Took would do well to have bonnets similar to that worn by pretty Pamela; at which opinion the Tookses bridled and looked venomous, while Mrs. Took remarked that men only noticed bonnets when they were on pretty women's heads: an impeachment to which old Took, monster that he was, pleaded guilty, with an unbecoming chuckle.

Among the humbler classes Pamela also found many admirers.

'That's a fine figure of a gal!' said Mr. Cobbles, at the coal-shed round the corner, to the wife of his bosom.

'You mind your taters,' responded Mrs. C.

At the grocer's shop, in High Street, where her mamma dealt, there was sometimes quite a scuffle between the two young shopmen as to which should serve her, although the Simpsons' orders were not very extensive.

When she was quite a little girl, and first went to Miss MacSpartan's, she won the gardener's heart by offering one day to tie a bow for him in a new red silk neckerchief. She never wanted for an apple after that.

One day Pamela had a few words with her sister—sweet girls! they often had these little contests when nobody but mamma, who did not signify, was present. And, after the row, the eldest daughter went out for a walk, by herself, in the Regent's Park.

She took a book with her and sat down to read; but the story was not very interesting, and, soon, her attention strayed from the work before her to other objects near at hand.

Under the head of objects, it would, perhaps, be unfair to class a fair-haired young man of rather rakish aspect, who wore a white waistcoat and a white hat, and was smoking a cigar; but it is very certain that Miss Pamela looked at him particularly. Now she could not very well help looking at this young man in the white hat, because, had she not done so, she must have dropped her eyes, or closed them, twice in three minutes, for, during that short space of time, he passed twice before her.

Of course, as would have been the case with any other young lady under similar circumstances, Miss Simpson never for a moment imagined that the person in the white hat was staring at her; and though, it is true, she looked at him, it must be added that she looked through him with that cold and icy stare with which a duchess might regard an omnibus conductor who had winked at her, as she passed by in her carriage.

The first time that he came between her eye and the distant landscape she noticed that he had a white hat on, without taking in any further details. The next time he passed she became conscious of a bright blue scarf and a cigar.

Two or three minutes afterwards—

'What a many white hats there are this season!'

Two or three minutes after this—

'It's the same man, I declare! What on earth is the creature staring at?'

He was certainly staring; indeed, to use the parlance in vogue among the bucks of a bygone period, he was ogling.

It is not the nature of young men, generally, to think themselves the least worthy of the human family. A young man, in a new white hat, may, surely, be pardoned if he courts, rather than shrinks from, public scrutiny. That lovely woman was created, wholly and solely, to succumb to the fascinations of the male eye, is, naturally, the belief of every fine young gentleman; and it must be allowed, however sceptical our fair readers may be on this point, that the most hopeless of male monstrosities does, somehow or other, without much difficulty, always find a member of the opposite sex to attach herself to his interests and take his cuffs and caresses with becoming meekness and gratitude.

When Miss Simpson quite made her mind up that it was she,

herself, who was attracting the attention of the owner of the white hat, a certain increase of sternness about her eyebrows ought surely to have been sufficient to show him that he had better go and stare elsewhere.

Perhaps it did show him that the young lady intended him so to understand; but he was a remarkably impudent fellow, and he continued the objectionable course of conduct which he had commenced. Nothing, surely, could have been more icy than the gaze with which the indignant virgin's blue eyes regarded him, as she rose, slowly, from her seat. Probably, never before or since did dyed silk rustle as did the dress of wrathful virtue, as it swept past him.

Oh! misguided proprietor of a white hat and blue satin scarf, ornamented with a golden horse-shoe. Why could he not have seen that his attentions were misplaced, and that his free-and-easy gallantry had better have been reserved for the gratification of the tender-hearted nursemaids, of whom, no doubt, there was a goodly sprinkling over the broad expanse of turf surrounding him?

But he did not. On the contrary, he pursued his wild career. He followed close upon the heels of the outraged beauty; he sidled up to her, and he said it was a fine day.

What did it signify to Miss Simpson what might be his opinion of the weather? Can the most unscrupulous of readers pretend to argue that, because it happens to be a fine day, a young man—although wearing a white hat and a scarf of blue satin, which may, or may not, have been decorated by crimson sprigs—should presume to communicate the undisputed fact to a fair and perfect stranger? If such a state of things were allowed to exist, it would be almost better not to have any fine days.

'Sir!' said Miss Simpson, in a tone which would have filled a well-regulated mind with dire alarm.

'It is such nice weather for a stroll,' continued this most audacious person in the white hat.

'I have not the pleasure of your acquaintance,' said Miss Simpson, growing momentarily more and more icy.

'What can so soon be rectified?' continued the lawless owner of the blue satin scarf. 'It is true that we are strangers; but when I look back at bygone years, and think that I have lived so long and never known you, I am absolutely lost in wonder. You ask me why?' he continued, inquiringly.

'I ask you nothing, sir; except it is how you dare to insult me?'

AUDACIOUS BEHAVIOUR OF SPRING GREEN.

'Insult you!' said the person in the white hat, seemingly much astonished. 'Not for worlds. If there is anything that I can do to prove to you how distant was such a thought from my mind——'

'If you do not immediately leave me, I will appeal for protection to one of the Park-keepers.'

'It is not because I am afraid of the Park-keeper,' said the white-hatted stranger, 'but I will wish you good-morning.'

He raised the white hat as he spoke, and bowed and walked away; and it must be owned that Miss Simpson could not help thinking that the Park-keeper's close proximity had a good deal to do with the free-and-easy stranger's rapid departure.

There was something like a faint smile of contempt upon Pamela's pretty face as she pursued her homeward course. It seemed to her, when she thought it over, that her admirers were singularly unheroic. Although there might be found among them an instance of a hero's soul, they all alike beat a rapid retreat in the hour of danger. All this was very unsatisfactory, and quite contrary to the pictures of life which she had studied weekly in a penny miscellany that she and another young lady at Miss Mac-Spartan's had subscribed to, each, in turn, defraying the expense every alternate week. Ah! but a hero really was a hero in those thrilling pages, and spent half his time, at least, in rescuing beauty in distress—in distress, it may be added, beauty in penny miscellanies generally contrives to be.

Why could not she, Pamela asked herself, find something heroic, at the nick of time, to come to her aid. Just now, there had been a good chance, if there had been a hero handy. He, with the white hat, might have been felled to the earth. Pamela might have fainted in the arms of her preserver, and, when restored to consciousness, have found that a coronet awaited her acceptance; which, in all probability, had nothing better turned up, she would have accepted, and lived happy ever afterwards. But the moment of danger had come and passed, and no hero had put in an appearance; and she could not help thinking that had the danger been greater, the hero might still have been absent in the moment of need.

It would be very delightful, she thought, to be rescued by the gallant scion of a noble house; but even the experience of the last few minutes was sufficient to convince her that it would not be safe to run great risks. The Regent's Canal was close at hand; but who could say with certainty that the Royal Humane Society's drags would come in time, much less the noble scion, who, for what she could tell, might be rescuing other beauty in another neighbourhood.

Very despondingly did our pretty Pamela bend her steps towards the Terrace of Daffodil, which, though undoubtedly quite as genteel as ever, she somehow found this morning to be much narrower, and more smoky than usual. She did not feel altogether equal to joining in a discussion then in course of progress in the front parlour, and having reference to the advisability of turning a grey linsey. Such like little economies struck her, at the moment, as being rather mean and paltry; so she went straight upstairs and had a good cry, and then washed her face and sat down to read one of Mr. James's romances.

Thus occupied, she did not hear a knock at the street door, a strange voice in the passage, or footsteps on the stairs; but when, presently, she went down to the parlour she found her mamma and Penelope in a great state of excitement.

'My dear,' said Mrs. Simpson, in a sort of breathless voice, 'we've let ——'

For a moment Pamela was inclined to treat the matter with indifference. She was not quite sure whether a heroine's family ought to let lodgings; but, in spite of that, she could not help feeling some curiosity on the subject.

'It's a single gentleman,' said Penelope; 'and he's to have his breakfast and tea and supper in his own apartments, and take dinner with us on Sunday.'

'His friends are all in the country,' said Mrs. Simpson. 'Where did he say he came from, Penelope?'

'I don't know, mamma; but he's in the medical profession; that is, he has not passed his examination yet, but he's studying at the Hospital.'

'He's a most quiet and gentlemanly young man,' said mamma; 'and, I must say, I think we're most fortunate, for he objected to nothing.'

And, indeed, it would have seemed as though this young medical gentleman were, really, a noble scion, in disguise, so reckless had he appeared to be regarding the price of the extras.

'Is he upstairs now?' asked Pamela.

'Of course not, my dear,' replied her mamma, in a tone of gentle reproof. 'It is necessary to be circumspect in these matters. As soon as your papa comes home this evening he is to go about the reference—though I feel quite sure that no inquiries are needed,—and this evening, at eight, Mr. Spring Green will bring his luggage.

'Will papa send to him, then, to say that the reference is all right?'

'Well, the fact is,' replied Mrs. Simpson, though this time less confidently than before, 'I omitted to ask Mr. Spring Green for his address; but, of course, that will not signify, as your papa could obtain it from his reference, and send to him in case, which is quite unlikely, it was not satisfactory.'

A little later in the day, however, it struck Mrs. Simpson that, as it was nice and fine, and a little walk would do her good, and the reference lived only in Gower Street, she might, herself, go round to make the necessary inquiries. She, therefore, made herself very smart, and, taking Penelope with her, set out upon her errand.

'A clerical gentleman, my dear,' she said, when afterwards describing the interview to Pamela, 'though with quite a military air—yes, quite military.'

'And the room smelt dreadfully of tobacco,' said Penelope; 'but he's been a chaplain in the army, and they all smoke in the army, you know.'

Evidently the ladies were quite satisfied with the reference, although the appearance of the Reverend Mr. Simple had not been altogether what they had expected to find it. When Mr. Simpson came home in the evening, he was much gratified by the intelligence that he had got an occupant for his drawing-rooms, who was, apparently, all that could be desired; and, the old gentleman having been bustled through his tea, the family were in a fever of excitement until the highly-desirable young medical gentleman arrived.

He came punctually at eight, in a four-wheeler, which was heavily loaded with his luggage—that is to say, there was one very long box and one very small carpet-bag; the long box being on the roof, and Mr. Spring Green and the carpet-bag inside. There was another person inside with Mr. Spring Green and the carpet-bag, who was, Mrs. Simpson said, the clerical gentleman before alluded to. A tall commanding person this proved to be, wearing moustachios,

NOT VERY MUCH LIKE A CLERGYMAN.

and a light drab coat and a white hat—which might not have looked as dashing without the mourning band that half covered it.

Both gentlemen were smoking when the cab drew up at the door; and Mrs. Simpson was visited by a pang of conscience when she suddenly remembered that she had said nothing upon the subject of tobacco to the new lodger, who, while studying for the medical profession, was quite capable of saturating the whole of the drawing-room furniture. He was in other respects, however, so extremely desirable, that she secretly determined to allow the smoke, if, when reasoned with gently, next day, he should refuse to give it up.

That portion of Mr. Spring Green's luggage which was contained in the small carpet-bag was, as the reader may suppose, very soon transferred from the cab to the house; but to get the long box off the roof, through the passage, and up the stairs was a process, tedious as regarded time, and damaging as regarded Mr. Simpson's wall-paper. As, too, the porterage of the box required the united efforts of Mr. Spring Green, his clerical friend, and the cabman, and there was a good deal of discursive talk among them respecting its safe disposal, a small crowd gathered in front of the house, and the arrival of the lodger was, evidently, the subject of remark among the neighbours.

Very little, therefore, had been gained by Mrs. Simpson's forethought in fixing upon twilight for Mr. Spring Green's arrival. However, the lodger had come, and Mr. Simpson and the ladies, taking turns to peep at him round the window-curtain, could, with the exception of the cigar, urge very little against him.

It is true that Pamela as yet had not been able to catch a glimpse of his face. About half an hour after he had come, though, she had occasion to go upstairs, and, when coming down again, had reached the drawing-room landing, when the drawing-room door opened suddenly, and she found herself face to face with the medical gentleman.

He had not at the moment got on a white hat; but there, sure enough, was the blue satin scarf with the crimson sprigs, and there was no mistake about its wearer being that very rude young man in the Regent's Park who had had the impudence to tell Miss Simpson that it was a fine day.

CHAPTER VIII.

EXTRAORDINARY BEHAVIOUR OF A SINGLE-MAN LODGER.

It has long since been decided by persons of wisdom that we should not judge by appearances. There are peers of the realm whose bearing is hardly noble, and linen-drapers' assistants who, out for a holiday, look like princes of the blood. Perhaps at a cursory glance the writer of this work might not be taken for a person of exalted genius; and though, of course, the reader is an exception, people somehow generally turn out ever so much worse than you expected, if you don't think the worst you can of them at first sight.

Although, when the climax came, Mr. Simpson was heard to assert that there had always been a something about Mr. Spring Green he did not quite approve of, his family expressed themselves quite positive that if he had had any misgivings he had kept them very carefully to himself. Mrs. Simpson, on the contrary, defended Mr. Spring Green to the last, and only gave him up, as a bad job, when his conduct became thoroughly outrageous. And it was not long in reaching this point, as will be seen.

Poor Pamela's feelings, when she caught sight of and recognized the audacious stranger, can easily be imagined. Meeting Mr. Spring Green's admiring gaze with an angry stare and frown, she swept past him and rustled downstairs, looking, outwardly, very fierce and unapproachable, but being, in reality, half-frightened out of her wits.

What was she to do? she asked herself, whilst pretending to partake of the evening meal, at which her unconscious relatives were assembled. How could she reveal the fearful truth to these poor happy innocent ones, who thought that Spring Green had come in the regular course of events, that he was going to be a model lodger, and they were going to make quite a nice little sum out of him for extras alone?

But she knew the truth. She knew very well that Spring Green must have followed her home, and knocked at the door in the hope of seeing her. Probably, then, it had occurred to him to ask, on the chance, whether there were any apartments to let, and thus it had come about that he was now the occupant of the first floor.

She felt quite certain of one thing, and that was, that Mr. Spring Green had come there, solely, upon her account. But what were his intentions? That was a question she found difficult to answer. And why had he brought that extraordinary long box? That was another, more difficult still.

But the most difficult question of all was, what was she to do? How could she tell the family what had happened? What would they say to her? Was not she always getting into some such scrape? She determined to keep her secret for the present, and say nothing, until it became positively necessary to speak.

While these reflections were causing Miss Pamela much uneasiness, the family were quite joyous with their future prospects. Out of coals alone, when the chilly nights came on, Mr. Simpson proved by arithmetic they would, if the lodger had only one scuttle a day, make upwards of two and fourpence profit.

'Hang it, though, that's too much, isn't it?' said Mr. Simpson, with a qualm of conscience.

'Not at all,' replied mamma, decisively. 'We're not supposed to let our apartments for the fun of the thing.'

Just before the conclusion of supper, there was a temporary check to the prevailing contentment. Hannah Maria came in to say that the new lodger wanted a pot of ale. Mr. Simpson looked over at Mrs. Simpson, as though in some uncertainty, but Mrs. Simpson said, with decision:—

'Draw the large white jug full, and take it upstairs.'

'Some of that in the cellar, mum?' said the handmaiden, doubtfully.

'Certainly,' replied Mrs. Simpson, and went on with her supper as though nothing at all out of the ordinary course of events had taken place. Mr. Simpson's countenance, however, might have been observed to wear a thoughtful and, even, anxious air, while, every now and then, he seemed to be listening.

Hannah Maria, meanwhile, went downstairs, then upstairs,

then came downstairs again, and, then, there was a brief pause. After this the drawing-room bell rang.

'Please, mum,' said Hannah Maria, appearing, presently, at the parlour door, 'the gentleman says he don't like it.'

'Don't like what?' inquired Mrs. Simpson.

'It's the ale, if you please, mum. He says I'd better change it, or go to a new shop.'

It had been calculated that the family ale, retailed at eight-pence or even sixpence a quart, would realize a very nice profit, and the disapproval of the new lodger was one of the last things expected.

Mr. Spring Green and his clerical friend partook of a couple of pots of ale, and then Mr. Spring Green's friend was reported by Hannah Maria to have said that he must be toddling. Upon this, according to the same authority, Mr. Spring Green had volunteered to put him in a line, and they had gone out together for this purpose.

'Has he got a latch key?' asked Mr. Simpson; and Mrs. Simpson replying indignantly in the negative, Mr. Simpson sat up to let the new lodger in.

He came home between twelve and one, and threw Mrs. Simpson into some alarm by letting fall his boots with a loud crash upon the landing.

'I hope he'll be careful about the candle,' she said; and several times, during the night, she sat up and sniffed, under the impression that she smelt fire.

Next morning the family were thrown into a fresh alarm, by Hannah Maria making a statement to the effect that Mr. Spring Green, when coming home over night, had forgotten the number and had knocked them up, by mistake, next door but one.

'It will be all over the Terrace,' said Mrs. Simpson; and so it was before the day was out.

Shortly after Mr. Simpson had gone to the city, Mr. Spring Green went away to his hospital, and mamma made a tour of inspection upstairs. There was no doubt about the medical gentleman being a smoker, and, already, to use Mrs. Simpson's expression, the window-curtains smelt like a tap-room. There was also a black spot upon Mr. Spring Green's pillow, which was suspicious, like what might have been caused by a spark. But, surely, it could not be possible that he smoked in bed.

You may be sure that all the doors and windows were set wide open, to get rid, as much as possible, of the lingering fumes of the narcotic weed; but, strange to say, when they seemed to have entirely evaporated, Mrs. Simpson began to sniff harder than ever.

'Hannah Maria,' said she, 'there's something extraordinary somewhere.'

The morning passed away without the occurrence of any event of an unusual character. Mamma and Penelope discussed Mr. Spring Green at great length, and arrived at the conclusion that they might have done much worse if there had been a chance of picking. But before the afternoon was over they began to feel uneasy.

A man came with three dozens of stout. It was evident that there would be no consumption of the family ale, even if, as had been contemplated, a superior quality were laid on for the purpose. A couple of dozens of soda-water also arrived during the day, the appearance of which awakened a vague suspicion in Mrs. Simpson's mind that Mr. Spring Green was not quite as steady as he might have been. Nor did the advent of the medical gentleman, himself, tend to reassure her; for he drove up in a cab, nursing a large earthenware bottle, and accompanied by his clerical friend, from whose pockets the necks of other bottles wrapped in paper were seen peeping.

'There's liquor enough to open a gin-palace,' said Mrs. Simpson, whose ideas respecting the consumption of strong drinks were naturally rather limited. 'But what on earth will they do with it?'

Presently Hannah Maria was in a position to give information upon the subject.

'He says he's got some friends coming,' she told the lady of the house; 'and he wants to know if we've got any spittoons.'

'Spittoons!' gasped Mrs. Simpson, who would as soon have expected to have been asked to provide double-barrelled guns or swimming-baths. 'What next?'

About six o'clock the friends began to arrive. There were half a dozen of them; they had mostly a jovial appearance; and all smoked. Mr. Spring Green, who was upon the balcony, called to them as they came straggling up the street, searching for the number of the house. Upon recognizing their host, some of them struck attitudes upon the pavement, and one, picking up a stone, made as though he was going to throw it through the drawing-room window. They were, generally, rather more frolicsome than Mrs. Simpson could have desired, who felt, instinctively, that the eye of the Terrace was upon her.

Going upstairs about half an hour after the company was assembled, Hannah Maria came down again, coughing violently, and observed that it was more than enough to choke a black. She also added that she never knew anything like that Mr. Spring Green's friend that came yesterday—he kept going on so.

It would have seemed—to judge by the noise they made—that all the company were 'going on;' and more than once Mrs. Simpson had serious doubts whether they were not coming through the ceiling.

Pamela and Penelope sat pale and trembling.

'I wish papa was at home,' said the eldest, looking wistfully out of the window. As yet Mr. Spring Green had made no further advances, and, indeed, seemed as though—if such a thing were possible—he had forgotten all about her; and this conduct only made her the more nervous. 'He'll burst out presently,' she thought; 'as soon as he gets tipsy—I'm sure he will.'

There appeared to be little doubt about their determination to enjoy themselves. 'I've ordered some oysters for nine,' Mr. Spring Green told Hannah Maria; 'get us some lemons and a heap of bread and butter, and that's all we shall want.' Then he added to his friends, 'Look here, you fellows, we're going to have a roaring evening!'

Mrs. Simpson and the young ladies were far from relishing the idea which this announcement suggested, for it appeared to them that there could scarcely be much roaring without the whole Terrace being alarmed.

'If I had only dreamt that there was to be anything of this kind, my dears,' said Mrs. Simpson, 'I never would have consented to your papa taking that young man Spring Green for a lodger; and what will happen next, and how it all will end, is really more than I can imagine.'

This was one of Mr. Simpson's late nights in the city—once a month he stopped to work until half-past eight or nine o'clock, so that it was more than ten when he reached home, generally very tired and with a bad headache.

He never felt more tired in his life than he did on this particular evening as he turned the street corner; but when he reached his own house, the unusual scene there enacting aroused him as effectually as if he had walked into a shower-bath and pulled the string.

The drawing-rooms were a blaze of light; the blinds were drawn up, and gentlemen in shirt sleeves were to be seen reclining gracefully in all varieties of attitude. The roaring part of the evening had evidently set in, and the gentlemen were wishing they were birds, at the top of their voices.

A small and admiring crowd, assembled in the street below, swelled the chorus, while, at the same time, they watched with interest the somewhat perilous progress of two gentlemen, evidently of the party, who were climbing from one balcony to another half-way down the street—a course of conduct which appeared to give dissatisfaction to some of the residents of the other houses, who came out at their drawing-room windows to argue with them, by the way.

'Is Bedlam broken loose?' was Mr. Simpson's inquiry, when, having fought his way up the steps, he got at last into his own house, and stood breathless and panting before the terrified ladies.

'Samuel,' said Mrs. Simpson, 'this is awful! The whole neighbourhood is aroused!—we are irretrievably disgraced! It seems there is another young man from a hospital lodging five doors off—at the Pilkington's, that we always thought such very superior people,—and he and the young men upstairs have been paying one another visits up and down the balconies.'

'And there have been two or three organs,' said Penelope, 'and some mountebanks standing on each other's heads, and the top one drank a glass of beer that Mr. Spring Green handed to him out of the window.'

'And they've sent in from the houses on both sides,' said Pamela, 'with their compliments, and they wish we wouldn't make so much noise.'

'There's only one course open,' observed Mrs. Simpson, in conclusion, 'and that is, Samuel, that you go upstairs and turn them out.'

At this Mr. Simpson looked thoughtful. Through the window he had caught a glimpse of a roomful of strong young men, all more or less intoxicated, and he did not see his way clear.

'Have you sent up any remonstrance?' he asked after a pause.

'We've sent up twice, but it seemed only to make them noisier; and we, who thought we could let our apartments so nice and quietly and nobody know anything about it, why we might as well have tried to hide a roaring lion as that young man, Spring Green!'

'Hannah Maria,' said Mr. Simpson, sternly, 'go upstairs at once to Mr. Spring Green with my compliments, and say that I shall feel obliged if he make less noise.'

'If you please, sir, I'd rather not,' replied Hannah Maria.

'What do you mean by you'd rather not?' inquired her master, with increased severity.

'Oh, because, sir, if you please,' answered Hannah Maria, with confusion, 'that friend of Mr. Spring Green's that came yesterday do go on so.'

Things, however, could not thus continue. The noise upstairs was growing, momentarily, louder. The company had had their supper, and somebody suggested pelting the crowd outside with the oyster-shells. By the bumping on the floor it would almost have seemed as though two of the gentlemen were dancing; one at the window, Hannah Maria stated, had kissed his hand to the housemaid next door but two, who had been sent out to fetch a Hansom. Indeed, things were reaching a climax, and Mr. Simpson resolutely buttoned his coat across his breast and prepared for the worst.

But upon the stairs he met Mr. Spring Green, himself, looking very flushed in the face and tumbled about the hair.

'Misher Whatsh-your-name,' said the new lodger, speaking with great determination, but some indistinctness of utterance, 'why, doosh! don't they bring hot watersh? Told Hannah Mariash, bring hot watersh—why, doosh! don't bring hot watersh?'

Detecting himself in the act of tumbling forward upon Mr. Simpson while making this inquiry, the new lodger straightened himself up, and, with even a greater show of determination than heretofore, repeated, 'Hot watersh! Misher Whatsh-your-name.'

'Mr. Spring Green,' said Mr. Simpson, taking the lodger by the arm, and regarding him sternly, while the young man, assuming an expression of supernatural intelligence, endeavoured to stand

A HOUSEMAID FROM THE TERRACE.

upright as he listened. 'Mr. Spring Green, when you took my apartments we had no idea there was to be anything of this kind, and it won't do!'

'That's all rightsh, ole fella,' said the lodger, nodding his head and frowning, while he winked both eyes violently to show that he quite entered into Mr. Simpson's ideas upon the subject; 'we won't do it any more, 'pon m' soul! Let's have hot watersh.'

'Not a drop, Mr. Spring Green,' replied Mr. Simpson, with resolution. 'Go upstairs, sir, and tell your friends to go away, or I shall send for the police.'

'WHO'S THAT CALLING 'POLICE'?'

Upon hearing this, Mr. Spring Green stared very hard at his landlord, steadying himself by the balustrade as he did so; then nodded to him mysteriously, and reeled back upstairs.

'I say, ole fellash,' Mr. Simpson heard him remark upon reaching the drawing-room, and by a loud crash which accompanied the words it was to be supposed that, in assuming his place at the table, Mr. Spring Green had tumbled on to it—'I say, old fellash, Whatsh-his-name says no hot watersh—Whatsh-his-name ought to know—No hot watersh!'

'Never mind the hot water, Green,' cried his clerical friend, cheerfully; 'we'll do without, first rate—let's have some cold.'

'Whatsh-his-name says too much row. Better hook it.'

'Oh! come, that won't do, Spring!' retorted the clerical gentleman. 'Why, this isn't half an evening yet! You aren't going to turn us out, surely?'

'Dear fella!' replied Mr. Spring Green, knocking over some glasses, so as to reach over and shake the speaker by the hand, 'stop for ever! Damn Whatsh-his-name! Hannah Mariash, bring hot watersh!'

'I'll put a stop to this!' cried Mr. Simpson, as soon as the yell of defiance which had followed Mr. Spring Green's reply had somewhat subsided; and, opening the street door, shouted lustily for the police, quite reckless, now, of what the Terrace might think upon the subject.

One of the force was luckily close at hand, and, though disturbed, perhaps, in the middle of an agreeable *tête-à-tête*, came, without delay, to render all the assistance that lay in his power. Unfortunately, however, this assistance was not very great.

He had no power, he explained, within a dwelling-house. If Mr. Simpson liked to lay hold of the lodger and his seven riotous friends, and throw them one after another down into the street, he had a perfect right to do so; but the police had no right to interfere.

'Do you mean to tell me that the only way I can clear my house is by pitching those vagabonds out of the window?' inquired Mr. Simpson, indignantly.

'Unless you turn them out at the door, that's all you can do,' replied the policeman.

Mr. Simpson was not, in a general way, inclined to acts of violence, but, under these desperate circumstances, he felt as though he had, suddenly, become possessed of the strength of Sampson, and, backed up by the policeman, he boldly ascended the stairs and faced the company.

When the British lion is thoroughly aroused, as everybody knows, his aspect is tremendous, and there was something about the expression of Mr. Simpson's eye which, doubtless, struck terror into the bosom of the revellers, for physically he was rather a feeble old gentleman, easily to be doubled up. Perhaps, too, the sight of the policeman's uniform in the background had something to do with it, for Mr. Spring Green's friends, after a momentary hesitation, began to look for their hats.

'Please to go away without any further disturbance,' said Mr. Simpson, mildly but firmly. 'And I shall be obliged if you will go too, Mr. Spring Green. You have not paid any rent as yet; and you seem,' continued Mr. Simpson, looking about among the fragments, 'to have done a good pound's worth of damage; but we won't mention that. There are also things that you have had to eat and drink. We shall be rather out of pocket by your visit; but that's our loss. Please to take yourself off, and we'll cry quits.'

'Misher Whatsh-your-name,' said Mr. Spring Green, trying to rise, and breaking another tumbler in so doing. 'I've been very comfor'ble and nothing complain of. Saw your daugtersh, shir, in park. Thought like come hersh. Devilish fine girlsh. No pology needed, Misher Whatsh-your-name.'

'We'll say nothing about apologies,' replied Mr. Simpson, who could not follow the youthful Green in his wanderings. 'Only please to take yourself and your friends out of my house.'

'Look here, Spring,' here observed his clerical friend, taking Mr. Green by the arm, 'the old boy puts it very properly. You're horribly drunk, or you'd agree with him. Take his tother arm, Jones, and we'll help him home to my lodgings.'

But it was not quite so easy to induce the new lodger to leave a house where, he assured them with tears in his eyes, he had been very comfortable. At first he suggested that his guests should depart, and that he himself should remain to spend a quiet evening with the ladies, and have a cup of tea and a little music. Catching sight of Mrs. Simpson on the way downstairs, he assured his clerical friend that she had been a second mother to him, and wanted him to give up smoking. After this he fell into a despondent state, as it occurred to him what he might be if he only did give it up, giving up drinking at the same time; and he apologized to Mr. Simpson for not being sober enough, now he came to think of it, to be able to appreciate the quiet evening he had previously alluded to. Visited at this juncture, however, by the recollection that, after all, Hannah Maria had never brought the hot water, he called for it afresh, and was led away, complaining bitterly.

Before going away Mr. Spring Green's clerical friend had promised to send the first thing in the morning for the luggage; and, now, nothing remained but for the family to pay a visit to the vacated apartments and estimate the damages.

'Though really why you should want to charge nothing for all that that young man has smashed to pieces, Samuel, is more than I can imagine.'

'If it had been twice as much,' said Mr. Simpson, 'I should have thought myself very well paid by getting rid of him; and if you're of my way of thinking this shall be the first lodger and the last.'

'I'm sure there's nobody was more opposed to the whole scheme than I was,' replied the good lady; 'but why we should not be paid for the breakages, when we have the young man's luggage still in our possession, is really more than I can understand.'

But when the conversation had gone thus far Hannah Maria came screaming downstairs, and, to the consternation of the family, fainted away in the passage. She had been up in the back drawing-room where the luggage was standing, and, the lid of the long box being unfastened, she had peeped in, and seen something which had thus alarmed her.

'It's corpses,' explained the horrified handmaiden; and, upon inspection, the long box was found to contain three-quarters of a subject, and about half a hundred-weight of bones, which, certainly, was a kind of luggage they had no wish to detain any longer than they could help it.

'And suppose he never sends,' said Mrs. Simpson; 'I'm not at all too sure that we may dispose of the things, even if we could get any one to take them off our hands, before we've advertised three times in the newspaper. And, before then, if we don't all have a fever, I shall be very much astonished.'

CHAPTER IX.

PANTATTLE: A MYSTERY.

'Mamma,' said the youngest Miss Simpson, about a week after Mr. Spring Green had taken his departure, 'I think I have found somebody who will take our drawing-rooms.'

'Bless me, Penelope, how's that?'

'It was at the stationer's, mamma,' replied the young lady. 'I had gone in for this week's *Quiver*, and I found him there asking Mr. Watkins whether he could tell him of any nice quiet apartments. He said he did not want them in a regular lodging-house, or anywhere where they would take his tea and sugar, or anything of that sort; but he would like a small private family that he could make one of, and he would prefer one that was pious and musical.'

'Certainly, my dear,' said Mrs. Simpson.

'And, just when he had got that far, mamma,' continued Penelope, 'Mr. Watkins caught sight of me, for I was waiting for an opportunity to give him the penny for the *Quiver*, and he mentioned to the gentleman that we had just exactly what would suit him. So then the gentleman took off his hat, and asked when he might be permitted to call upon you on the subject. You've no idea, mamma, how very gently he speaks. I'm sure he won't turn out like that dreadful Mr. Green.'

'There's really no answering for anybody,' said Mrs. Simpson; 'but we can only try, my dear, can we? And when did you say he was to come?'

In half an hour's time there came a very soft double knock at the street door, and, after a preliminary ahem, a very mild voice inquired of Hannah Maria, dry-polished for the occasion, whether Mrs. Simpson were visible. A reply having been given in the affirmative, there followed a great deal of very careful boot-wiping, and, picking his way across the hall and up the stairs, the visitor left between Hannah Maria's finger and thumb a card, on which was engraved the single word—

PANTATTLE.

'Bless me!' said Mrs. Simpson, when she had very carefully examined the pasteboard, not only the right way up, but upside down, and, then, from each side. 'It's just like one of those checks they used to give your papa and me at the theatre when we went out between the acts.'

FIRST APPEARANCE OF PANTATTLE.

When the good lady had given a hasty touch to her cap ribbons, she went, smiling, upstairs and found a bald, grave gentleman, seated in an easy chair, in the drawing-room, who proved to be the Pantattle above referred to.

He certainly was one of the gentlest gentlemen Mrs. Simpson had ever met with, and, really, opened the negociation with so much delicacy, not to say hesitation, that Mrs. Simpson almost began to be afraid that he expected to get his board and lodging for nothing. When the necessary arrangements had been made, Mr. Pantattle took his departure, after fixing the next afternoon for his arrival.

'I only hope we shall get on all right,' said Mr. Simpson, when he heard what had been settled upon. 'I expect there have been

AS IT USED TO BE.

some people who have dropped into the middle of a family circle and rather surprised them.'

'The fact is, Samuel,' said Mrs. Simpson, 'if you had your way you would just have us all bottled up like a lot of vinegar plants, and see nobody but ourselves from year's end to year's end; and that's exactly how it is that when you do go out into society you don't know how to behave yourself.'

'I shall take care not to go,' said Mr. Simpson.

'Bah! I haven't common patience to hear you,' said his good lady.

Mr. Pantattle's luggage was neat and unpretending. It consisted of a portmanteau and a writing-desk. There was no attempt at show about him.

'I never wear anything but what you see,' he said, the first evening, alluding to a black suit which was not in its early gloss, 'and I have no watch.'

He said this, too, with a kind of air which seemed to imply that there was something highly reprehensible in a person's carrying their own time about with them; and Pamela felt guiltily conscious of a showy gold chain which papa had given her on her last birthday.

In many respects Mr. Pantattle was peculiar. When asked if he would partake of muffins, which figured on the table, in honour of his arrival, he replied: 'We are not for long here, madam. Why not?' Which observation seemed to Mrs. Simpson to have something of the character of a riddle, and she would have wished him to repeat it again slowly, only she did not like to ask him to do so.

She felt rather nervous, too; for when they first took their seats, and, just as she was in the act of raising the teapot to pour out the first cup of tea, Mr. Pantattle laid his hand gently upon her arm and staid her further progress, whilst he asked a blessing; a proceeding which also caused some embarrassment to the head of the family, who, at that moment, had a mouthful of muffin which he could not, well, dispose of until the blessing was over. Throughout the meal Mr. Pantattle was very calm and grave; and, excepting that he ate and drank rather more than all the rest put together, manifested few signs of human weakness.

He knew nothing of the city, he said to Mrs. Simpson, and very little about money matters. 'I have enough, and seek not to increase that which I possess, nor to imperil its safe keeping.' Upon the subject of ladies' dress he had a remark or two to make. He thought it was better and more simple as it used to be, and it would grieve him very much to see any one he had a respect for following the fashions; an opinion at which Miss Pamela tossed her pretty head. Mrs. Simpson, speaking of him afterwards, said he talked like writing lessons in small hand. To the Misses Simpson he was bland and courteous; but the effect of his politeness was, upon the whole, depressing. Mr. Simpson felt immensely relieved when he could get away from the table, and he made his escape under the pretence of having something to look for among his papers.

After tea Mr. Pantattle sat bolt upright in an arm-chair by the window, and the conversation wearing itself out, very gradually, he fell into a gentle doze. Aroused from this by a suggestion on Mrs. Simpson's part that the lamp should be lighted, he protested mildly against shutting out the day, and the poor ladies acquiescing, meekly, they sat three-quarters of an hour longer in the twilight, and Mr. Pantattle fell into another doze in which Mrs. Simpson, this time, bore an audible part.

Shortly after eight, the new lodger sought his chamber, and a rather tedious evening thus concluded.

'I rather think Pantattle will be one too many for us,' said Mr. Simpson; 'but we'll give him a fair trial.'

He was easier to bear with next night, perhaps because the strangeness had worn off a little; and nothing occurred to break the even monotony until the lamp was lighted, when, drawing a leather-bound volume from his pocket, he said that, if not disagreeable, he would like to read a chapter.

'Make yourself quite at home, sir,' said Mr. Simpson, in the innocence of his heart, little dreaming what was coming; and, thus encouraged, Mr. Pantattle read them a chapter of Job, and, kindly, explained his notion of its meaning.

'I rather think,' said Mr. Simpson, when, once more, they had said good-night to the new lodger, 'we shall have to get rid of Pantattle.'

Next night, when the young ladies were at the piano, he expressed a desire to try his voice, and sang a hymn or two. Mr. Simpson had formed a desperate resolution if he offered to expound again;

but he did not do so. Indeed, he seemed light-hearted and almost frolicsome, this evening, and entertained the ladies with an anecdote and some tricks with a piece of string. When he was gone, Mr. Simpson observed—'Pantattle's coming out.'

'You always take such violent prejudices, Samuel,' said Mrs. Simpson. 'I'm sure he's, really, most inoffensive.'

A week wore away, something in this fashion, Mr. Pantattle remaining in-doors almost all day long, and receiving and writing a good many letters, which, latter, he took to the post himself. It was evident that he had a good deal of business, of some kind or other, to transact, although he knew little about money matters; and Mr. Simpson, who had been told by the reference that Mr. Pantattle was an independent gentleman, wondered not a little what could be the cause of such an extensive correspondence. Presently, the explanation was forthcoming.

There were some gay young dogs and rollicking blades at Kooter and Phlimsy's, who met other gay young dogs, from other banks, at an hostelry in Bucklersbury, whereat they partook, in company, of their mid-day meal.

'Say,' said one of these rollicking blades to another, one morning, whilst eating his steak and reading the paper, 'doesn't old Simpson, at our place, live at No. —, Daffodil Terrace, Gloucester Gate?'

'I think that was where I sent him his letters, when he was away for a holiday,' replied the person addressed.

'I'm sure of it,' said the first speaker; 'and here's one of the rummest capers you ever tumbled to.'

With which words the first rollicking blade handed the second one the newspaper, pointing with his finger to a particular advertisement.

'It can't be the old man,' said the second rollicking blade, when, after a few exclamations of astonishment, he had calmed down a little, and read the advertisement for the second time. 'He would never venture to do a thing like that. Why, the bank would no more stand a game of that kind than they would his opening an opposition shop in our lobby.'

'Suppose we have a shy at him. Then we shall find it out

easy enough. Look here; let's write an answer, in a sham name, and give an address where they'll take the letter in.'

'That's your sort; let's do it as soon as we get back.'

'I'm on.'

That afternoon, therefore, a mysterious despatch accompanied the other letters posted from the bank, to which an answer was received during the course of the next day; and a long consultation ensued between our two rollicking blades, out of hearing upon the staircase, the result of which was as follows:—Mr. Simpson, returning to his desk after a momentary absence, found an envelope lying there, awaiting his arrival, on which his name was written in a hand he did not know. Opening the envelope, he found a sheet of paper; and unfolding this, he read, in blank astonishment, these remarkable words: 'HOW IS PANTATTLE?'

For several minutes Mr. Simpson sat, silently, with the paper in his hand, feeling extremely unwell. Then he glanced furtively around, to see who it was that could have played him this trick. The bank was the last place where he would have wished the fact of the lodging-letting to be known; but, evidently, the secret had oozed out, somehow, and the question was, Who had found it out?

He passed the rest of the afternoon uncomfortably enough; but, yet, poor gentleman, he little dreamt how matters really stood, nor could Mrs. Simpson, when he related the circumstance, throw any new light upon the subject. Next day, though, he found another envelope, which contained an advertisement clipped from a newspaper, and gummed upon a piece of paper; reading which, he was seized with a sudden giddiness, and felt as though he must have fallen backwards off his stool, had he not clung to the desk for support. Then, seizing his hat, he staggered rather than walked into the manager's room, stammered out something about a domestic calamity, and hailing a Hansom cab at the street corner, bade the man drive for his life to Daffodil Terrace. His advent there, under these circumstances, caused quite a sensation; and the young ladies flew to the door to welcome him, with a vague impression that somebody must have left some member of the family a legacy. But the expression of his face soon convinced them of their mistake;

and he put them on one side as he asked, in a strange hoarse voice, 'Is that man upstairs?'

'Mr. Pantattle, papa?'

'Yes ——'

'Oh! Mr. Pantattle never goes out in the day,' said Penelope. 'He's very busy, always, and says nobody is to disturb him.'

'I think I'll disturb him, though,' said Mr. Simpson, doubling up his fist.

'Oh, papa! what's the matter?'

'Go into the parlour, both of you, and don't come out till I tell you. I'm going up to talk to the lodger.'

When Mr. Simpson reached the drawing-room, he found Mr. Pantattle seated at the table, writing a letter. He evidently did not expect company, though, for he was seated there in his shirt sleeves, and his shirt was of flannel and very much out at the elbows.

'Do you know anything of this?' asked Mr. Simpson, laying a piece of paper on the table. It was the advertisement above referred to, certain derisive commentaries attached.

'A private gentleman of property,' ran the printed words, 'having a few thousand pounds at his disposal, will be glad to lend the same upon good personal security.—Address, per letter only, enclosing stamp for reply, to Mr. Pantattle, No. 9, Daffodil Terrace, Gloucester Gate.'

'Are you the gentleman of property, may I inquire?' said Mr. Simpson, eyeing, rather suspiciously, Mr. Pantattle's general appearance, which, certainly, did not give an impression of much spare capital.

'My dear sir,' replied Mr. Pantattle, smiling blandly; but yet not, altogether, without a certain uneasiness in his expression; 'you have guessed rightly.'

'Perhaps so,' said Mr. Simpson, sitting down and laying his hand very heavily upon the table. 'You don't know much about business, you said the other day. Now, I know a little, and about your business, particularly. I won't go into the question of the liberty you have taken in using my private address for your advertisements, without first consulting me upon the subject; but

PANTATTLE: A MYSTERY.

EXIT PANTATTLE.

I'll come straight to the point. Please to take what belongs to you and go about your business, or I'm damned if I don't kick you out into the street.'

If ever there were an expression of blank astonishment depicted in a human countenance, it was depicted, then, in that of Mr. Pantattle; but Mr. Simpson's quick glance told him that with that astonishment was more of fear than anger, and that, after the first surprise, the capitalist's next idea was how to save himself from the threatened violence.

'You—you would not think of resorting to any such measures, sir, I trust,' said he, with a weak attempt at virtuous indignation; 'and you'll please to remember you've engaged to board and lodge me for the week, and there's to be a week's notice after that.'

'You're welcome to your board and lodging so far,' said Mr. Simpson, wrathfully, 'for I wouldn't soil my hands with your money; but you'll take yourself out of my house this very moment, or, by Jove, I may do you an injury.'

'My dear sir,' said Pantattle, putting on his coat, in a great tremble, 'after what has occurred I could not think of staying any longer under your roof. But I cannot go without observing that this is not the way one gentleman should act towards another.'

'Don't you talk about gentlemen,' shouted Mr. Simpson, scarlet with rage. 'Do you think I'm such a fool that I don't read all your trumpery swindle? Do you know the name of Robert Fondilove, may I inquire? I don't know and don't care a deal whether you do or not, but I'll tell you this much. Just such another pack of lies as these you've printed here got a bill of exchange out of a poor old friend of mine, and when he died cost me near two hundred pounds to settle, though he never got one penny piece for his paper. You may not be a bill stealer, Mr. Pantattle, but I'll be ——' (here we are sorry to say Mr. Simpson swore again, though it is not much to be wondered at) 'if I believe you're a man of property; and, so, I'll give you the benefit of the doubt, and not kick you out, if you go quietly.'

Something, though, stronger than himself, took possession of Mr. Simpson's right boot when Mr. Pantattle, standing upon the landing, ventured upon a feeble threat of legal proceedings, and the owner of the spare thousands made the descent of the stairs more rapidly than he had calculated upon, and sprawled like an ugly black beetle upon the mat.

But here a wholly unlooked-for episode took place; for, when Mr. Simpson followed Pantattle downstairs, his youngest daughter flung herself before him, and besought him, passionately, to stay his arm.

'You shall not raise your hand against him, papa,' cried the excited young lady. 'You shall not. You shall not. You shall not.'

'Why, what on earth do you mean, my dear? I'm more likely to spoil my boots on him! Here, Martha; look here, I say. Why, the girl's going to have hysterics! Now, you, sir, clear out, or it will be the worse for you. That's right!—shut the door, Hannah Maria; there's an end of that vagabond.'

'Vagabond!' said Mrs. Simpson. 'Will you please to explain?'

'All in good time, my dear,' replied the master of the house; 'look after Penelope first. Had you any notion that there was anything?—but there's no accounting for girls' fancies. Anyhow, thank God, we're in time to put a stop to it.'

'So much for our second lodger,' said Mrs. Simpson, just before she went to sleep that night.

'Second and last, if I have my way,' said her partner; but in less than a month the drawing-room was let again.

CHAPTER X.

TATTIMAN IN HER NIGHTCAP.

It happened in this wise.

One bright summer's morning, a middle-aged young lady—somewhere upon the sunny side of fifty—wearing a green gown and a blue bonnet, and carrying a dilapidated parasol and small brown-paper parcel, knocked a double rat-tat at Mr. Simpson's door, and looked down his area. The head of Hannah Maria there appearing, for

LOOKING OUT AFAR.

the purpose of taking observations, and retreating again with confusion, upon being detected, the door was opened, and the middle-aged young lady informed, in answer to her inquiry, that Miss Pamela Simpson was at home.

It was her old friend, humble Miss Tattiman, who had come

MERMAIDS AT HERNE BAY.

to see her dear pupil; and you should have been there to see the meeting! As regarded Tattiman, nothing could have been more ecstatic. For weeks, for months,—it seemed like years—she had been longing to see her Pamela, and at last her dearest wish was fulfilled. At the same time, too, she had found an unexpected pleasure—the pleasure of making Pamela's mamma's acquaintance.

'Oh, my dear madam, your dear daughter is absolutely, if possible, far prettier than ever!' cried the gushing Tattiman, clapping together as she spoke a very old pair of green kid gloves, ever so much too long at the finger-ends. 'She was the belle of our school when she was with us; but what is she now? I have a sketch of her among my treasures, done by an old friend of hers—you recollect that dear Topsawyer girl, Pamela. It is you, my dear, at a balcony, with an opera-glass, looking out afar—though I forget what it was you were looking for; do you remember, my darling?'

While thus she chatted pleasantly, humble Jane Tattiman's eyes —good, serviceable eyes, though not a pretty colour—took in many details connected with the Simpsons' domestic economy. If she had had any vague idea of disposing of a certain small packet she had brought with her, carefully sealed up and labelled a diary, and a few letters, or something of that sort, she changed her mind before the visit reached its conclusion. Before that time arrived she had learnt that the Simpsons had lodgings to let, but no lodger.

She was herself without a home at that present moment. This was the holiday-time at the MacSpartan establishment, and the young ladies had gone to the sea-side. Tattiman had had some idea of being a mermaid at Herne Bay, but had changed her mind. Besides, she had other matters to think of. The MacSpartan and she had parted—there were limits to the endurance of a packhorse. *That woman* had heard the truth about herself for once, and Tattiman hoped she had liked it. When Mrs. Simpson was so pressing, how could Tattiman help stopping to lunch? On the contrary, she stopped and ate heartily.

A day or two afterwards, there came such a brisk rat-a-tat-tat at the street door that the ladies were thrown into a gentle flutter of excitement. Who should it be but Tattiman, and more excited than the ladies. She did not dare to tell them her errand though;

she was so afraid that they would think she was taking a liberty, and Tattiman was one of those persons who would rather die than do such a thing. When encouraged, however, by the assurance that they knew her to be all she said of herself, and a good deal more besides that was sweet and amiable, Tattiman told them that she had an elderly male relative of the name of Bodgerby, a rich single gentleman, who had come up from the country, and wanted some quiet apartments.

So desirable a person was this Mr. Bodgerby, according to the account which Miss Tattiman gave of him, that Mrs. Simpson saw, at a glance, here was exactly the kind of lodger they had so long been looking for; and, indeed, when, in the course of the following day, he arrived with his luggage in Daffodil Terrace, he appeared to be quite as desirable as he had been depicted. He was one of those lodgers whose bill was brought to him, by his express order, every Monday morning at half-past nine, and paid, the moment he received it, with no further examination than a glance at the total.

He was one of that sort, too, who did not want to see anything more of the fragments of yesterday's meals, when they had once left the table. He had a way, too, of bringing home little presents for the ladies of the house, which was not a disagreeable trait in his character; as, for instance, when he bought himself some asparagus in Covent Garden, he would send home a second bundle for the Simpsons.

Before the end of the first week, he had taken mamma and the girls to the dress-circle at the Haymarket; and when, in return, they asked him to dinner on Sunday, he sent in three parts of the dinner himself. He did not board with them, but had such a number of delicacies for his breakfasts and suppers, and sent so much away untasted, that it was, really, as much as the family could do to prevent the good things being wasted.

'Upon my word,' said Mr. Simpson one day, while in the act of eating some Strasburg pie, 'this sort of thing is really quite—quite prodigal!'

The second week he was there, there was more holiday-making —a box at the theatre and a trip to Hampton Court.

'He is liberality itself!' said Mrs. Simpson, when relating the particulars of these high jinks and junketings to humble Tattiman; and humble Tattiman assented, with a quiet smile. She knew more of her relative than this worthy family, and knew him to be not quite so unselfish as they supposed. They, too, in due time, found that Mr. Bodgerby's liberality was of that order which includes itself in the treat. He was a very rich old gentleman, and, any day, when the fancy took him, would have paid the expenses of a tableful of good company; but a starving wretch whom he passed by on his way to the banquet would have supplicated vainly for a penny.

'I like something for my money,' he remarked, on one occasion. 'I don't mind paying dear; but I like something for my money.'

Jane Tattiman had, long ago, endeavoured to negociate a little loan from her wealthy relative, but had tried in vain. Finding he had come to town and wanted lodgings, she had recommended those of the Simpsons', because—but surely we need not seek for a reason when the desire to do a friendly act so, naturally, suggests itself as the most probable.

She was just at that time, as we have seen, without employment, and often looked in upon the family in Daffodil Terrace; who, feeling themselves to be under no small obligation to her, were only too happy to give her a kindly welcome; and she, frequently, took her place at their table, and even slept beneath their roof, when, the time slipping away unobserved, it was all at once found to be too late for her to catch her omnibus.

But she did not make one of those pleasure parties before mentioned, and, strange to say, Mr. Bodgerby did not care for much of Jane Tattiman's society.

Thus time wore away; Mr. Bodgerby being even more liberal than usual, and Tattiman calling quite as frequently, and, occasionally, helping mamma and the young girls with their needlework; for they went out so much now that constant changes in their toilet were necessary. The new lodger had been with them more than two months when, one day, Mrs. Simpson asked herself a question.

They were going to the theatre, that night, and Pamela was dressed and ready to start, and Mr. Bodgerby stood looking at her whilst she fluttered her fan, unconscious of his attention.

'Does he mean anything?' Mrs. Simpson asked herself, and subsequently asked Mr. Simpson the same question.

'Nonsense!' said that gentleman. 'The idea of such a thing! He's much too old.'

'I'm not so sure of that,' said mamma, after due reflection. 'He certainly is much older; but really for my part I have no

'DOES HE MEAN ANYTHING?'

patience with your very young men, who, half their time, don't know their own mind. Besides, really, with such an income.'

Only a night or two after this remark was made, however, Jane Tattiman saw Mr. Bodgerby helping Pamela on with her opera cloak, and all the way home, that evening, in the Waterloo omnibus, she sat up in the corner, looking very grim and thoughtful.

'I hope,' said she, addressing the looking-glass, when, having reached home, that night she sat facing it in a highly unbecoming nightcap, 'I hope you've not made a fool of yourself, Jane Tattiman. You may come into something, if nobody comes in between and cuts you out, when that old wretch has eaten himself into another world; that is, you may, if he doesn't leave it all to a charity, which he is very capable of doing. Now, look here, Jane Tattiman, what you've got to consider is, what will be the best thing for you. You're no beauty, Jane, and you're never very likely to get married yourself. Pamela Simpson is a fool, and might easily be managed. You might, perhaps, find a comfortable home under her roof, if that old wretch does not quarrel with you, or you might sell those letters to advantage. Yes, decidedly. The creature any day might find a wife, and one of his own picking. Why should he not have one that you picked? He shall, Jane Tattiman. The future happiness of the interesting lovers rests in your hands. Jane Tattiman, your blessing is required. Lord love your long nose! What a hobby-my-goblin you look in that nightcap!'

Next morning, quite early, Miss Tattiman paid her rich relative a visit, and, when he came into the breakfast-room, he found her waiting for him, her bonnet and shawl on a chair beside her. To tell the truth, he looked more surprised than pleased at this matutinal visit; but he was more amiable than usual, and asked her to have some breakfast. Jane said she didn't want anything. Then she stood looking at him a moment. Then made a rush at him, caught his head between her hands, and, shaking her nose at him playfully,

'Oh, you sly old boots!' said she. 'I've found you out, have I?'

As he expressed some surprise, she told him, then, that she knew his secret, and that he had fallen in love with Pamela.

'Do any of the rest of them know it?' asked Mr. Bodgerby.

'Of course they do, you old silly,' said the playful Jane.

'Oh,' said Mr. Bodgerby.

Somehow there was something rather funny about Mr. Bodgerby's manner that morning, and, when Jane Tattiman went away, she half wished she had been more cautious in opening the negociation. She and the Simpson ladies went out a walk in the Regent's Park that afternoon, and the matter was discussed at some length;

'OH, YOU SLY OLD BOOTS!'

but when they returned home they found Hannah Maria with an enormously long face.

'Oh, if you please, mum,' said she, 'he's gone.'

'Who's gone?' asked Mrs. Simpson.

'Mr. Bodgerby, mum,' replied Hannah Maria, and handed Mrs. Simpson an envelope addressed to her. Opening this she found a ten-pound note, and the words 'I will send for the difference,' written inside. He had taken away some of his luggage, leaving the rest locked up; but nothing to give a clue to his whereabouts, or the reason for his sudden flight.

'It's scandalous,' said Mrs. Simpson.

'It's astonishing,' said Miss Tattiman.

'It's all your stupid meddling,' said Mrs. Simpson; and the two ladies straightway had a quarrel upon the subject.

'Don't ask me to help again, that's all,' said Miss Tattiman.

'I never did ask you.'

'You may do yet.'

'I don't think it.'

'We shall see.'

And Tattiman retired with a toss of the head and a scornful sniff.

CHAPTER XI.

THE LAST OF BODGERBY.

How strangely things do come about. Who could have dreamt, when old Bob Fondilove lay dying in that ill-shaped room in Clement's Inn, that the Simpsons would ever have come down to letting lodgings! Who could have dreamt that a lodger of theirs would ever come to live upon the self-same landing, and that, under any possible combination of circumstances, Jane Tattiman and our pretty Pamela should chance to pay him a visit upon the same day!

Surely, little better than the ghost of a lodger was that which humble Jane found, stowed away there, in a little stived-up room—a wan and haggard ghost, with a ragged grisly beard—the shadow of that Bodgerby who used to partake of such a profusion of good things in Daffodil Terrace.

Nothing like the old voice, which she so well remembered, was the weak treble that bade her enter; and, for a moment, she started back, affrighted, by the ghastly figure, in the dingy dressing-gown, crouched by the side of the fire.

'You didn't expect to see me, I suppose,' said the visitor, coming forward.

'I didn't want to,' answered Mr. Bodgerby.

'No doubt,' observed Miss Tattiman, with a grim smile. 'There's no love lost between us, I dare say. I've come on a matter of business, that's all.'

'Get through it and leave me,' said Mr. Bodgerby, without much waste of politeness.

'Very well, then, this is it. The Simpsons are bringing an action against you for breach of promise of marriage, and the cause is to be heard to-morrow. Am I right so far?'

'I believe you are.'

'Do you suppose that they have got any case against you?'

'I suppose so, or they would not try it.'

'Well, I think they cannot do much, unless I help them. I'm not very well off, you know, and I can't afford to stand in my own light. But I would rather be on your side, Bodgerby, if it's worth your while to make it worth mine. Now I've got here a little packet of papers—a diary, and some love-letters, and such like, which might be of some use to you if we can come to an arrangement.'

It was about four o'clock in that winter's afternoon when Tattiman took her departure, and twilight was gathering in the distant corners of the room and out upon the silent staircase. When the laundress came, presently, to light the gas upon the stairs, she, also, lit a candle for Mr. Bodgerby, and asked him whether he wanted anything.

'No, thank you,' he answered, 'I'm all right. Don't bother.'

'That old man gets more of a brute, every day,' was the worthy woman's reflection, as she closed the door behind her.

Left to himself, he sat, silently, by the fireside, gazing in a dreamy way upon the dying ashes. When, after a while, he rose from his seat to put on some coals, he almost lost his balance.

'I'm very ill, I suppose,' he muttered. 'I haven't the appetite I used to have; that's what's wrong with me. To-morrow I must send for a doctor.'

He went back to his seat and fell, again, into a brown study, still gazing on the smouldering embers. But, presently, he pressed his hand to his head and murmured some words, confusedly. Then, rising, he, with great difficulty, fetched his desk from the other side of the room; and, drawing the candle towards him, began to examine his papers, tearing some up, and flinging others into the fireplace.

Near upon nine o'clock, a young lady, who had ascertained from the porter which were Mr. Bodgerby's chambers, slowly ascended the crooked stairs and knocked, timidly, at the door.

'Perhaps he is out,' this young lady thought to herself, 'and I may not have the opportunity of acquainting him that this is not my doing, that it is all that horrid woman's fault, who has persuaded and misled mamma and papa. Oh, I must see him and tell him that I will not go into court, and beg his pardon and pray of him not to despise me for what has been done.'

OUTSIDE THE DOOR.

When, however, Pamela had knocked two or three times without receiving any reply, she ventured to open the door. Something seemed to warn her, then, that she was on the eve of a terrible discovery; and she paused, irresolute, her hand pressed to her heart, listening. At last she went forward into the silent room.

He lay, there, dead, with his head on the table, and the papers he had been destroying scattered around; among which were a young lady's diary and some dog-eared love-letters, dated from North Brixton. His hand clutched a document having the appearance of a legal instrument, and which, when examined, proved to be his will; but none could say whether or not that, also, would have been destroyed, had not death thus stayed the old man's hand. When his lawyer, in due course, came to read it, he, as well as many others, was much surprised, but there was no reason for supposing it not to be genuine.

'It's an extraordinary world,' this gentleman observed. 'The old fellow must, actually, have loved the girl after all; and her family, somehow, must have bungled matters very strangely. However, Miss Pamela Simpson is pretty sure of a husband now, with fifteen hundred a year.'

But did she ever get married? Ah! that is a question to be, hereafter, solved. The adventures of Miss Simpson are, with the reader's kind permission, to be resumed at an early date. If her history thus far has pleased you, the writer can confidently promise, next time, new scenery and dresses, and something very thrilling in the way of plot.

'I made a pretty good thing by those letters,' thought Tattiman to herself; 'but I sold them to the wrong side after all, and if she's only found out the truth, there's good-bye to all my chances of getting anything else out of Miss Pamela.'

'I wonder what the Terrace will say now,' was Mrs. Simpson's observation. 'I saw them turning up their noses, and I haven't forgotten it.'

'Supposing he had left the money to me,' thought Penelope.

'Supposing I had thrown myself away upon that chemist's assistant,' thought Pamela; 'and yet ——'

'Fifteen hundred a year!' thought Hannah Maria, whose wages were twelve pounds per annum; 'I wonder whether anybody ever spent as much.'

'What a world it is,' thought Mr. Simpson, on his way to town outside an omnibus. 'I, really, never supposed our Pamela would have cut such a figure.'

THE END.

EDWARD BAINES AND SONS, PRINTERS, LEEDS.

www.ingramcontent.com/pod-product-compliance
Lightning Source LLC
Chambersburg PA
CBHW020126170426
43199CB00009B/661